Op(

Beyo:

Introduction.

In 1982 an intelligence mission onto the Argentine mainland failed before it had started. Operation plum Duff was the daring reconnaissance mission to gain vital intelligence of aircraft and Exocet missiles as well as troop deployment at the Rio Grande airbase, but the mission failed and no information had been obtained, and with a short time frame the Mikado mission for a raid on Rio Grande had to be abandoned.

The Special Air Service were then under considerable pressure to launch a mission to attack the airbase at Rio Grande. At the time, no intelligence was available on the base, no one knew what troops were based there or even what aircraft were using the base.

In the book The Sixth Seat I told the story of how a one man mission was engaged to get a man behind enemy lines and to gather the vital intelligence that was needed before any mission could be planned.

However, the mission was authorised by some rebel officers within the Regiment who thought that operation Mikado and the bold raid of Rio Grande would only be a suicide mission.

The one man mission behind the enemy

lines had proved three things, and that was that the airbase was a lot busier than at first thought, and two there were also Exocet missiles at the base and they were being carried by four Dassault Super Etendard jets. And finally, three, the base was a hell of a lot better defended than anyone had thought

The single mans intelligence reports had also indicated that positioned around the base area were not just conscripted troops but also Marines as well as the highly skilled Argentine special forces Buzo Tactico.

The plan to land two C130 Hercules onto the runway at Rio Grande, would also be hampered by Argentine radar and also radar controlled gun emplacements around the airfield

The plan to land up to fifty SAS men on the airfield had now begun to fade and as time went past the threat from the Argentine air force was starting to decline.

However, this story will look at an alternative to the original plans of the mission and could have changed the whole history of operation Mikado.

This book is dedicated to Len, I hope that you enjoy the read. And to all the men who went to the South Atlantic in 1982.

All names are fictious and the story all though based on facts is a fiction story of how Operation Mikado could have been well carried out.

OPERATION MIKADO

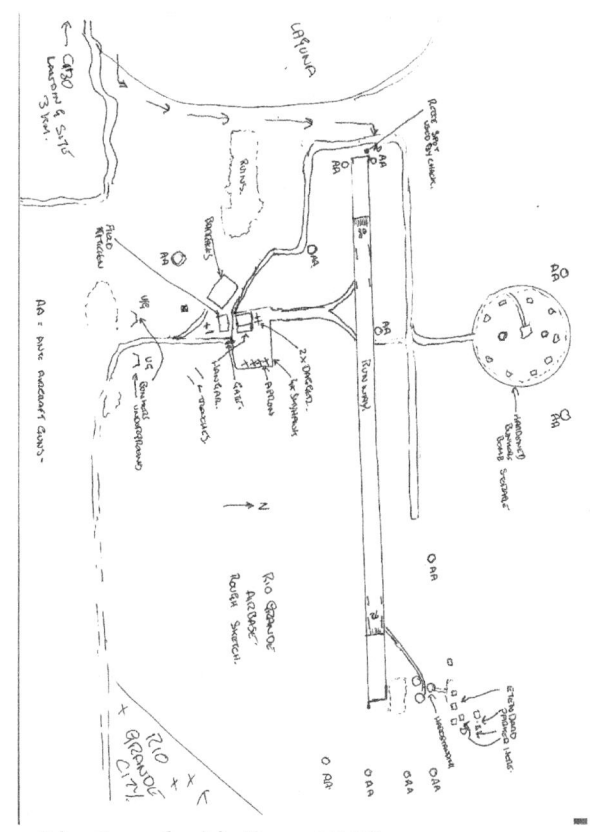

Rio Grande Air Base 1982

CHAPTER ONE

RAF Lyneham 22.30

Two C130 Hercules transport planes were loaded up with men and equipment from the SAS Regiment.

The aircraft once loaded taxied to the runway and prepared for there take off. The men onboard the C130 were fully equipped with weapons and a full bergen for there mission. They will be deployed at an unknown airbase and their mission would be to eliminate all troops and to seek and destroy four aircraft that are parked at the airbase. They would then either return to the two C130 Hercules aircraft or if that were not possible, they would carry out an escape and evasion exercise too a safe position that would be given to them at the airbase that they are going to attack.

All information on the target airbase was to be kept to a minimum, the purpose of the exercise was to place the men in an unknown environment with an unknown continuing situation, this way the men would have to think on the ground and to face any problems as they arise.

The two Hercules were now cleared for take

off and they both had now taken to the air; the pilots and crew knew where the target airbase was, but this was kept from everyone.

The two Hercules were cleared to drop to minimum hight during the exercise and all information was kept as secret as could be allowed, taking in the fact that they would have to be aware of civil aircraft and that civil aircraft would have to also be aware of their location.

The two Hercules turned just after taking off and dropped down to a low level taking them up north towards the Bristol channel. They then followed the Bristol channel up towards Gloucester and then headed north west of the Malvern hills keeping there level as low as possible and keeping both aircraft as near to each other as possible, the second aircraft around one hundred feet higher to avoid any turbulence.

The two aircraft then followed the Teme valley north west towards Ludlow. During this time, the SAS men inside the aircraft were settled down and not enjoying what had turned out to be a bumpy ride, as the aircraft were flying as low as they could, this meant that they had heavy turbulence from being in changing air, the ride so far had felt like a bumpy coach trip, in fact a few men even had their paper bags at the ready just in case.

The two Hercules had now turned west towards Newtown in mid Wales and started to cross over some of the mountains in the area, once they had reached Newtown they would then turn north west and head towards Dinas Mawddwy, it was here that the two aircraft slowed up slightly, and now they dropped down even lower, in fact so low as it would attract a number of complaints about low flying aircraft nearly taking the chimney off a few houses.

The two aircraft had no turned off any navigation lights and were now flying completely on night vision googles, they were also using other pieces of equipment that they had gaffer taped to the dash board of the instrument control panel.

Meanwhile a couple of the SAS men on board who were lucky enough to be next to a window were now trying to work out their location from the stars above when they could be seen.

The two aircraft had now begun to twist and turn around the bends in the valleys that they were following, and this came at the annoyance of the SAS men who were now feeling there evening meals starting to rise.

The two Hercules aircraft followed just above the A470 road towards the Cross Foxes Inn, they then overflew the Cross Foxes Inn at ultra low level and headed towards Dolgellau and then heading west along the Mawddach river towards Barmouth bridge.

The two Hercules had now dropped even lower, and the ride was now even more bumpy.

**

Llanbedr airbase, North Wales 23.30.

At Llanbedr airbase a company of infantry

soldiers were spread out at various locations at the airbase. The men had been briefed on an exercise that they may be attacked during the night by unknown soldiers, rumours were ripe amongst the men as too who might attack them during the night, and also if this was leading up to them being shipped down to the South Atlantic and the Falklands islands.

The mission for the combat infantry was to defend the airfield and also a number of mobile radar units that had arrived belonging to the royal radar establishment.

The night so far had been a mild evening with the occasional break in the otherwise cloudy sky that exposed the bright stars above them.

The airbase itself is situated less than one kilometre from the sea in Cardigan Bay, the main runway runs from north to south and is just over two kilometres long and the base has two other runways, one from north east to south west and at just over one kilometre long and the other at north west to south east at just over one kilometre long.

There are a number of small buildings at the north end of the base with some large hangars, and the radars have been located on the grass areas around the base at several places and have sections of combat infantry around them for protection.

Near too the hangars at the north end of the base are a group of officers, who are here to witness the exercise as it evolves in front of them. One of the officers was believed to be the DSF the Director of Special Forces UK, along with a few high ranking army officers who were also joined by and Air Chief Marshall from the RAF.

The men were stood together and were not doing much talking, they were all watching out for something out into Cardigan Bay.

At 22.45 the first hint of anything happening was from the sound being blown up on a south westerly breeze of an aircraft approaching the airbase, the flat ground that the base was situated on, and the mountains to the north and east meant that any approach would have to be from the sea both to the north and the south, and the sound that they could hear was from the two C130 Hercules that had just flown in from RAF Lyneham.

The aircraft so far were undetectable by eyesight the pilots of the two Hercules were down as low as they could go, and they were hugging the coastline from Barmouth upwards. The officers seemed to be confident that they could get two Hercules into the base undetected, but then they were then passed the bad news, the radars had picked them both up coming in towards the base from six miles out.

'Blast, the bloody radars,' the Director said as he heard the news.

'Shall we abort sir, now that they have been tracked,' One of the officers asked.

The Director took a deep breath and shook his head, 'No let them carry on, they will have to do the mission and go into the escape and evasion stage, we will have to take it the two C130, s would be destroyed.'

The two Hercules came in and landed on the long runway and made there way too the north end, no sooner had they stopped than a force of soldiers ran from the rear of the two aircraft and formed up and moved in towards the four aircraft had been parked up.

There was weapon fire with blank ammunition being fired, now all around as the Combat infantry moved in from their positions to challenge the invading force and the silent night was now awakened with the sound of rapid gunfire all around. The SAS soldiers put down a vicious return fire as they made their way towards the two hangars, a large number of thunder flashes exploded in the area of the four aircraft to indicate that they had seek and destroyed the aircraft as to there mission. The SAS men now put up a fight to clear the area and now with their new orders they were off into the darkness and heading towards the mountains to the east and there pick up point that they would aim for, the whole mission took twenty minutes the aircraft were destroyed but the two Hercules had to be declared as destroyed as well.

The Director was still hitting the roof, the plan for Mikado was a good plan, it could be done but the Achilles heel in the mission was how to get two C130, s down on the ground at the base without being destroyed, so far, they had no intelligence as to what radar was on the Rio Grande airbase and what troops to expect, as far as they know the Argentinians may not even have any radar at the base, but so far, they did not know anything.

'Blast that bloody aborted recce mission, if they had got to the airbase, we would have known what we were up against,' The Director was saying over and over again.

The Air Chief Marshall came over to him, 'I am sorry for the outcome, we will go through all this in the morning at Northwood,' he said as he patted the Director on the shoulder.

All the men on the base were now called in, the Combat infantry did an excellent job to defend the base and the radar teams did an excellent job although they were not being appreciated at the moment for the outcome.

The two Hercules had now turned around and were heading back out to sea and back to RAF Lyneham.

The SAS men had a meeting point ten miles away and they all arrived safe and well at the point and were then transported back to Bradbury Lines in Hereford.

CHAPTER TWO.

The Debrief, Permanent joint headquarters. Northwood. 10.00 the next day.

The debriefing room was full of high ranking officers from all services that were currently involved in Operation Corporate. The highest item on the agenda was the fact that Exocet missiles were still the highest threat to the fleet in the south Atlantic and now that the days are coming towards the eventual outcome that the ships would have to go inshore to disperse the troops for the land war to begin.

It was assumed at this point, that the Naval war that they expected was now unlikely to happen as Argentina had now pulled there ships back to the mainland because of the direct threat from the British nuclear submarine fleet and even their carrier the Veintcinco De Mayo was no longer a danger to British warships, but the main danger still existed from the Argentine air force and the Exocet missiles that were being launched from the mainland.

The Argentine air force have so far proven themselves as a potential threat, there pilots seem well trained, and they have proven that they can attack at extreme low levels if they need too.

The total lack of any ariel surveillance aircraft by the fleet means that they are almost blind to an incoming ariel attack. Gone are the days when the carrier fleet had their own Fairey Gannet AEW3. 'It may have been bloody old but at least it worked,' one of the officers shouted out during the start of the debrief.

The threat was on the ground in Argentina, they would have to knock out the Exocet threat and the sooner the better, if one of the Argentine aircraft had a run on a carrier then the war would be lost.

The men all argued for the first thirty minutes and then all went quite as all eyes turned on the Director who was sat at the table with three of his SAS officers by his side. The debrief went into the details of the previous nights mission in North Wales.

The Director also pointed out that his attacking Squadron were actually on the ground at Ascension island ready to go in if they need too and attack the base at Rio Grande,

'The four seven squadron crew from the exercise last night are also on there way into Ascension now and should be on the ground withing the next few hours,' the RAF Air Chief Marshall said as the room went dead quiet, and all the men listened in.

'And what about intelligence on the mentioned bases,' an Army Brigadier said as he took a sip from a glass of water.

The Director took a deep breath and then answered, 'With the failure of operation Plum Duff we have been looking at a way too put another team on the ground but so far we have not come up with anything,'

'What about a submarine,' one of the officers said.

'The water is too shallow in that area to get in near enough,' A naval officer replied.

'Parachute them in,' was another suggestion, but again that was pushed away as the aircraft would be detected as they came near to the land.

Again, the Navy were asked if they could provide another helicopter but again this was dismissed as the navy had only a limited amount, of helicopters that it could use and maintain onboard the ships, with the loss of the one that they donated to operation Plum Duff they were now having a job to maintain the fleet that they have, and they would need every helicopter that they have in the landing phase of the operation.

After the exercise in north Wales they had highlighted just how vulnerable an attack on Rio Grande would make both the SAS men and the two C130,s. One other way would be to move a team of men in from Chile over the border into Argentina and onto Rio Grande, the plan looked feasible but the men inside of Chile were too far into the north and the time scale to move them down south would be in days and they needed information now and not later also the government in Chile would not agree to a mission being mounted from inside there country.

The arguments and ideas went on for a number of hours, the meeting broke up for lunch and then was due to return with ninety minutes to discuss other ways of dealing with the problem of the Argentine air force and the Exocet missiles.

On returning too the meeting room a few of the officers that were there in the earlier meeting had now left and a few more had come into the meeting to replace them. Again, the agenda was taken up with the threat against the fleet and how to avoid any such attack.

One of the plans on the table was a bold attack by RAF Vulcans. The attack would involve one or even possibly two Vulcans, it was revealed that a Vulcan had actually flown close to the Argentine coast line a few nights back and had used its counter measures to try and block out the Argentine radar. With that and the fact that a Vulcan bomber in various positions is also a very stealthy aircraft, it was possible that the aircraft could go in at low level and either use Shrike missiles against the radars or it could even bomb the airbase.

The idea of a Vulcan bomber going into Argentine mainland and carrying out a bombing mission was at first welcomed but with some Ministers in the room it was cautiously being pushed off the table.

'Gentlemen, can you imagine the outcome of a potential nuclear bomber hitting mainland Argentina, no Gentlemen this will have too be taken off the table the consequences of this would be political suicide,' one of the Ministers answered, he also went on 'and none of this idea must ever be mentioned to the Prime Minister, do I make myself clear,' he said as his eyes darted around the table to make sure everyone had heard what he had said and would not repeat what had just been said.

So, the RAF withdrew their idea with the Vulcan, a pity as the aircraft would have been capable of carrying out the mission and would have been the best outcome to the situation.

The Director was now feeling the pressure again as many questions were being raised why a special forces team could not go in and gather the intelligence that was needed for any mission. 'It was their job to do this work, which is why we have them,' one Naval officer barked across the table.

More ideas were being placed on the table and the Director was looking at the clock on the wall, all this arguing, four seven squadron had their aircraft at accension, and the SAS had their men sat there, if only they could get over the issue of getting an aircraft in there, they could have done the raid by now.

They were now a good one hour into the discussion and the arguments for and against were being bounced back and then someone said something that made the whole room halt, and a silence went through every man in the room.

The Director looked across at a Group Captain that was sat on the other side of the table, 'what did you just say,' he asked.

The Group Captain looked around the room at all the silent faces staring at him and waiting for his answer, he could feel his face burning as he turned a bright red, he took a deep breath as he answered, 'what about the man that you guys put near Rio Grande the other night,' he answered, he thought to himself when he had answered, there I have slipped up and said it now.

The Director was sat there staring at the man 'what man' he asked.

Again, the Group Captain could feel all the eyes on him as he answered, 'the one that was dropped from the Vulcan.'

One of the officers in the room laughed at the idea, 'dropped a man from a Vulcan, what ever next,' but he was quickly spoken down by the Air Chief Marshall who scowled at him when he spoke 'be quite man, this was not impossible, the Vulcan is capable of carrying one or even two men and making a drop.'

The Director raised himself out of his seat, his officers that were sat around him quickly got up from there seats with him, 'get me the Ops officer at once' the Director shouted as he made his way along the room and towards the exit door. As he left the silent room again erupted into chatter again. The Air Chief Marshall had now lifted from his seat, and he too was on his way towards the exit to catch up with the Director.

The SAS operations officer at Northwood was not in the meeting at the time, he was busy concerning another operation in the South Atlantic and he had just finished a small conference call.

The operations officer at Northwood was Colonel Leonard Cecil, a man in his mid-forties who had been in the Regiment for the past ten years, he was a highly respected member of the upper sheds staff within the SAS Regiment.

Colonel Cecil was surprised when the door of the conference room he was in swung open with a bang, he turned around to meet the eye of one angry Director, but Colonel Cecil was not one to be intimidated by anyone not even a high ranking officer, so he gave the Director a glare back.

'what is all this about a man being on the ground at Rio Grande,' the Director demanded to know.

Colonel Cecil gripped the back of the chair he was standing behind that was parked neatly under the large conference table, 'Ah, I presume you mean the mission that Colonel Thomas had put together.'

'I do not care who put it together, but I have just been made to look a fool of, by the joint chiefs over a mission I did not know existed or knew anything about.'

The Air Chief Marshall now arrived at the

room, and he stood just behind the Director and his three men looking over at Colonel Cecil who was on the other side of the room behind the table, Colonel Cecil was not about to be hung out to dry over this mission, so he began to explain to the Director why the mission went ahead in secret.

'Listen Sir, Colonel Thomas and some others within the regiment were very anxious about sending two Hercules aircraft and sixty men into an airbase that no one had any intel on whatsoever,' Colonel Cecil paused for a moment and returned a glare at the Director before he continued, 'when Plum Duff failed, and the talk that Mikado will still go ahead a lot of the officers had an uneasy feeling, no one knew what was on the ground at Rio Grande and no one could guarantee that the two aircraft would not get shot down before they even landed, that is why they took the chance to put someone on the inside.'

'So, this someone, has he sent back any important intel,' the Director replied with a sarcastic tone.

'Only Colonel Thomas knows the answer to that.'

'Where is Colonel Thomas now.'

'Bradbury Lines as far as I know,' Colonel Cecil replied.

'Then get him here now, I want to see him.'

'I will arrange a car to collect him.'

'A car, get a bloody helicopter over to Hereford, I want him here as soon as possible,' the Director replied and at that he turned on his heel and headed back towards the Joints chief meeting.

The Director followed by the Air Chief Marshall and the three other special forces officers returned to the Joints Staffs meeting and retook their seats.

'My apologies gentlemen, it seems that we have a secret, secret mission that even I have not been informed about,'

**

Colonel Thomas took the Call at the SAS headquarters at Bradbury lines in Hereford. The Colonel had been informed that the Director had just gone nuclear and that a helicopter would be there at the base within thirty minutes to take him direct to Northwood.

'Well, it looks like the shit has hit the fan, the Colonel said to Squadron Sergeant Major Snow just after he had taken the call.

'Do you want me to come with you sir,' Snowy replied.

'No, I will fall on the sword, the rest of you just deny knowing anything about what we have done.'

'I do not mind taking the fall with you Sir,' Snowy replied.

'You keep yourself safe Snowy, don't get caught up in all this mess, I will see if we can find our way out of it, but it sounds like the boss is spitting for blood.'

The Gazelle helicopter arrived at the rear of

the base and landed, Colonel Thomas was all ready and waiting and as soon as it landed, he ran over and climbed onboard, and the Gazelle lifted off and turned over the base and headed south east.

**

The meeting at the Joint Chiefs of staff was adjourned for a few hours while they all went about their various duties and also while the Director awaited the arrival of Colonel Thomas from Hereford. The Director had calmed a little and was now put in the picture about the Vulcan mission by the Air Chief Marshall, but the Director was a little miffed that the Air Chief Marshall knew about the drop and the Director himself was left out of any knowledge of the event.

Colonel Thomas arrived at Northwood in the late afternoon and was escorted to an office where he was greeted by the Director and by Colonel Cecil the SAS operations officer at Northwood. Colonel Thomas was a short thin man in his early fifties and wore dark rimmed spectacles, to look at him you would never think that he was part of the SAS Regiment, but to know him you would find that he was one of the most, toughest soldiers that you could ever meet.

'Good afternoon,' Colonel Thomas said as he entered the office.

Both the Director and Colonel Cecil returned the welcome.

'Well, I suppose that I have some explaining to do,' Colonel Thomas said as he took a seat opposite the Director,

'Yes, you bloody well have,' The Director replied.

Colonel Thomas looked up at the Director, and then back down towards the desk before he began to explain, 'well Sir, after the failure of Plum Duff we were left with a vast hole, a hole that could not be filled, we had pressure from above that Mikado will have too go ahead even without any intel on the base,' The Colonel looked up now at the Director and took a breath before he continued, 'well myself and others became worried that without this intel then the mission could end in a complete disaster and not only would it cost the lives of good men it would also knock morale for six within the task force.'

The Director did not shout as he had earlier, he listened to Colonel Thomas, and he gave the man the respect that he was due.

'Tell me about this man that you have at Rio Grande, has he learnt anything as yet.'

Colonel Thomas leant down and pulled up his dog eared leather briefcase, it was the type of leather briefcase that looked like it had been around since the Colonel had been born, he opened the case up and pulled out a file and placed it n the desk in front of him and then opened it up.

He then sat himself up slightly and made himself comfortable in his chair and then opened the file and removed some papers.

'Okay, my man on the ground is a young Corporal, he has not been in the Regiment long and we grabbed him in between his training, we then tried to arrange transport to get him into Argentina but with the time frame we had we could not get him there fast enough,' Colonel Thomas paused for a moment and took a drink of water and then continued, 'Anyway as luck would have it we fell onto some information that the RAF were doing a probing mission along the Argentine coast near to Rio Grande, but unfortunately they were using a Vulcan bomber, so we thought that would be the end of it, but we were then informed that the Vulcan had a spare seat that they used for a engineer to travel in the aircraft when it went overseas, we were also told that the aircraft could drop a man by parachute from the entrance and exit hatch because the three man crew in the rear of the cockpit would use this hatch for any escape if they have to bail out of the aircraft.'

Both the Director and Colonel Cecil looked on and were now intrigued in the story so far.

'Well, we took the opportunity and pushed the lad into a mini bus to Brize and then down to Ascension just in time to board the Vulcan on the secret mission.'

'Fascinating, so all this I take it went to plan and we have a man on the ground,' The Director replied.

'Yes, Sir it was a success, and they dropped the man near the sea shore just a few miles south of Rio Grande, and then the Vulcan turned and carried out its own mission.'

'So, you have a man on the ground and what has he come back with, I suppose not a lot at the moment,' The Director asked.

'Well, he has been there two days so far and so far, he has come back with a lot of information, a hell of a lot that we did not know about the airbase, for starters the area around the airbase has a large detachment of Marines, there are also members of the Argentine special forces near the base,' the Director was looking up at Colonel Cecil, this was news to them both.

'And then we have the gun emplacements around the base, there are two gun emplacements on the western end of the runway at the end, and one each side, there is another one on the north side of the runway, and there are a number of emplacements on the eastern end of the runway, and on the beach that runs along there, we think these are the radar guided guns, there are also about a Company of men stationed at a small barracks, these look like conscripts, and there is a large gun emplacement on the south western side of the base, there is also two underground bunkers on the southern side that houses the officers and communications, there are also a number of radar anti aircraft weapon systems at the base,' Colonel Thomas paused for a few moments and looked at the Director and Colonel Cecil before he placed another sheet of paper on top of the ones he had just read out. 'And we come to the aircraft at the base, it is used by many visiting aircraft C130, s a Neptune AEW, there are four Dassault super Etendard aircraft on the eastern end of the runway, and they are hidden sometimes around the houses, there are also four Dagger aircraft and four A4 Skyhawk aircraft stationed at the base, and in the main hangar there are a number of missiles believed to be the four Exocet missiles.'

Silence fell in the room as the three men thought about the information, the Director took a deep breath, and then he rested his chin on his hands as he placed his elbows on the desk in front of him, he then answered, 'the threat with four Exocet missiles was still there, your man could actually go in and destroy them,'

Colonel Thomas gave a slight smile as he answered, 'unfortunately our man was sent in unarmed.'

'What, why did you send him in unarmed,' the Director replied with a scowl.

'We did not want too suddenly create an international incident with a shootout.'

Colonel Cecil cut in before this conversation turned into an argument 'so there is no way we could land any aircraft at the Rio Grande airbase.'

'Unfortunately, no,' Colonel Thomas replied.

'Is there anywhere else we could land, say on the beach,' the Director asked.

'We asked our man the question, but he said the sand on the beach was really lose soft sand and it also had hidden rocks in it.'

The three men sat their thinking for a moment, then Colonel Cecil asked 'Is there not any roads that a C130 could put down onto near the base.,

'Well, we have not got that information so far, all we do know that only the main roads around, and also out of the town are tarmac roads the rest are just dirt tracks, but we can always aske the lad the question.'

The Director looked up at Colonel Cecil and asked him, 'if we could get a Hercules in there away from the base, would it be possible to launch a raid and take out the Exocet missiles and the four Super Etendard aircraft.'

'It would have to rely on complete stealth and speed to do so, we would have to sneak in there as fast as possible and hit the base hard and fast and be back out fast.'

'Okay then, get to it Len, let us see if it can be done, and gentlemen we have the men on the ground at ascension and the aircraft all ready, we just need the okay and we will launch. But we need to sort it fast,' The Director looked at his watch, 'Colonel Thomas it should be dark in Argentina soon can you get your man to have a look for a landing spot, if at all possible, to put a C130 onto it,'

'I will send him a message now and get the lad onto it,'

'Good let us get moving and see if it can be done.'

As this the meeting was broken up, Colonel Thomas could breathe a sigh of relief at least he did not have to fall on his sword just yet. He now went to the signals room and gave one of the signallers the contact details for his man in Rio Grande and a message was sent out, *Urgent, look for somewhere away from the airbase to land to C130 aircraft, a road or a piece of flat ground..*

CHAPTER THREE.

Rio Grande Airbase.

Corporal Chack was just thinking about going around to the cook house to see what he could get to eat, going around there had its risks but he knew he could mix in there and get some hot food and also to see how the morale was going with the Argentine troops that were there, the cook house was a mine of information, just sit inside away from the Argentinians and listen to their conversations.

Chack looked all around it was just getting dark, and he would slide down the bank from his position on the west end of the runway and make his way around to the cook house tent and have a nose around the base as well. As usual the rain had started to fall again and he could feel the rain dripping down the back of his neck, it will be another cold wet night, he thought to himself.

The banter from the two gun emplacements that were just in front of Chack at the of the runway was in full swing, with bread rolls being thrown across the runway at each other as well as finished cigarette butts being flicked through the air like red tracers, and then landing on the ground with a shower of sparks.

It was now dark enough for Chack to slip down the bank, and down to his bergen and then just give the radio a check. As he checked the radio, he could see that a message had been sent and was in the memory, he placed his code into the radio and got access to the message that asked him to check and see if there was anywhere near to drop a C130 onto.

'For fucks sake I have told them, there was nowhere to land around here' Chack said to himself.

Chack looked around and over towards the west of the airbase, he had been on the edge of the area but not wondered off too far into the west. He decided that he would have a stroll over there and have a good look around, night time would bring him a lot of hours to spare and he could use the time doing something constructive.

First, he thought about the kitchen he could just nip in and get a feed and then out and about looking around, he decided that the kitchen was a good bet as he looked forward to a good hot meal and an hour would not make tonight's mission any difficult.

Chack walked around the base like he normally did and went and got some food in the field kitchen. He found that sitting in here for an hour was a field of informant gathering, he could learn a lot about what troops were in the area, and also what was going on, on the Falkland Islands. Not only that but the food was also good.

Chack finished his meal, and then left the field kitchen and made his way around the back of the base to collect his bergen and make his way towards the fence on the west side of the airbase. Keeping low and slow he made it to the fence, and then checked the road, and then sneaked over the low fence and crossed over to the other side.

There was a turn off along here he thought, the one that he walked along before and he headed towards it, once he had found it, he turned and started to walk along the road. The road was made from compressed rock and dirt, it must have started off as a dirt track at some point but then over time they had dropped small rocks into it and compressed it into some kind of smoother surface.

Chack started to walk on looking around in the dark for a landing area but looking at the land in the darkness was not much help, there are fields around, but they seem to be lumpy with chunks of grass growing in them. The land also looked flat but there were slow rises in the area as well and also lose gravel that could get kicked up, they were also very boggy with small pools of water.

Chack could remember the road he walked up that looked straight it moved from north to south but the ground between the road and the base may be too level and would pick up anything on radar, but it was worth a look just in case. Chack walked the three kilometres to the road and turned along the junction and followed the road. The road was narrow and was not so compact, and as he walked along the road, he came to a number of real deep potholes in the road full of water.

Okay, you could possibly bring a Hercules down on this road, but the pot hold was really big, what happened if you hit one, he thought as he used his feet to test the hole, he thought. The hole was deep and too deep to drop a Hercules down here and risk doing damage too it and having to abandon the aircraft and run for Chile before the mission had started.

Chack looked around and decided there was also the problem of a radar signature, it was still a bit close to the airbase and would be picked up flying around. Chack took a deep breath and checked along the road a little bit more, the road was just as bad the more he walked down it. He shook his head and decided to abandon this route and return back to the route at the junction.

It was now real dark and out here there was no light pollution so darkness out here meant real darkness, Chack walked on towards the road and came back to the junction, he looked along the road that headed west and thought to himself that the road must lead to Chile, he would have a quick look anyway.

Chack followed the bend in the road, the one good thing is that there does not seem too be much traffic along here at night as he had not seen any vehicles so far, he walked on and followed a long bend in the road, he could make out some low hills just in the not too far distance towards the north.

Chack walked along too yet another long bend in the road and followed it around all the time he was looking at the surface of the ground around him, he needed to find a flat surface without anything sticking up, and that was on hard ground, and not anything soft. There was no fear of anything sticking up as there were no trees too be seen up along here just grass growing, but hard ground was another thing.

Chack came to a straight bit of road, maybe this was long enough to drop a Herc onto he thought to himself but then he looked over to the east and could still see the areal towers at the Rio Grande base, the Herc would have to be driving along the road like a truck to get under the radar he thought.

He walked on along the road and came to a slight hill in front of him, his eyes had now adjusted really well to the darkness, so that he could now see a lot more around him, he could see slight lifts in the land giving slight inclines over a few feet, just a little bit more and they could drop a Herc behind it, he thought.

Chack looked up the road towards the small incline and thought that maybe he was wasting his time and should go back to the airbase for the night, he stopped on the road and looked around, there was no chance of anything landing here never mind anything the size of a Herc, he thought.

Chack looked again and then thought he may as well walk to the top of that incline and then turn around and head back. He walked on and it had now stopped raining, and the wind was still howling as it always does here, and the clouds had thinned a little exposing a few stars.

Chack had reached the top of the small incline. That will do he thought, but as he looked towards the west, he could see that the road was still dead straight, there were a few slight inclines here as well. Chack thought for a moment about just how far west did this road reach in a straight line. He decided to walk on a bit more and see just how much road there was.

Chack walked on for another two kilometres, the road was dead straight and then came too a few slight curves. He now measured out the width of the road to see if it was wide enough for a Herc to drop the under carriage onto the road, there was thirty feet, there was a camber in the road but not too much, he then checked the width to the fences, there were drainage trenches to each side of the road and wire fences a good way off the side of the road, Chack checked his rough measurements by foot and worked them out he had one hundred and fort one feet from fence too fence at the side of the road, so far there was no road furniture, he then measured the width of the road itself and that was thirty feet.

Chack walked back towards the base and he

checked all along to make sure that the road stayed the same width and also the fences, he needed to make sure that there was nothing sticking up like a road direction sign or anything on the ground that could be dragged up by a turboprop and thrown into an engine.

So far so good, he had to check that the incline could, if possible, block out any approach on radar, also if there were any turning points so that they could turn a Herc around to take off and head west after the mission, so far things did look good but then a gentle reminder appeared, a set of bright lights came over a slight brow on the road and then a truck came through from the west thundering past Chack, and heading towards Rio Grande. The most unpredictable part of any plan, humans, and traffic, no one could tell if a car would be coming along that road.

This would be an issue if they do bring an aircraft onto this road, they would have to leave the road clear of any vehicles so that would mean blocking it off somehow, without attracting attention. Chack, waited for the truck to vanish into the distance before he went back onto the road, he now carefully walked the road to make sure that any parts were not lose and could flick up and damage one of the aircraft' he also checked the sides of the road for any road furniture that may prevent the aircraft from landing and also to make sure that all the fences are at the same distance and do not come over into the road.

Chack, also had to check on his Magellan GPS for reference readings so that the pilots would have an idea where the road was in the dark, so that they could land. He found a number of road direction signs along the route and gave them a bit of a shake, one was loose, but the next one seemed to be cemented into the ground, he spent thirty minutes swinging on this to try and pull it over and eventually he managed to push it so it dropped down half way too the ground, he then hoped that this would be enough to clear anything on the Herc.

The only other draw back was the fact that he could not find a turning point, there was one gateway at the western end of the road that a Herc could possibly turn around on the junction to the gate but other than that there was nothing else.

The other problem was the fact that the ground in the ditches on each side of the road was wet and soft, so no vehicles could use it, but in some places, there were a few raised areas that seemed to use underground drain pipes, and these areas seemed firm enough for a vehicle to drive over the top.

Chack now set up his radio and sent a message, 'I have found a road west of the airbase four kilometres long, one hundred and forty one feet wide (estimated) and the road itself thirty feet wide (estimated), no road furniture, hard packed stone road solid.'

Chack sent the message and then waited for

a reply and as he waited, he had another look around, the best place he could find on the road was actually a dip, this would give some cover for any aircraft landing on the road.

CHAPTER FOUR.

Northwood.

Colonel Cecil had taken a bit of time out to grab some sleep in one of the living quarters within the large bunker, he had just been awakened by the orderly Sergeant 'Colonel, sorry to disturb you sir, but Colonel Thomas has asked for you in the ops room, he has just received a message from Rio Grande.'

Colonel Cecil lifted himself off the small bed and got up, he checked himself over to make sure he was presentable, and then made his way out to the ops room to meet up with Colonel Thomas.

'Hello Bill, I have been told that you have received a message,' Colonel Cecil said as he entered the room, the SAS ops room was a room with a number of large desks, each desk had maps and charts laid out on the desk, on the white washed walls there were notice boards with papers and photographs pinned to them for various missions that were currently being carried out by the SAS. The room was well lit, and Colonel Thomas was stood behind a desk looking at a large Atlas with the page turned to Argentina.

'Ahh, Len come on in, we have just received a message from our man in Rio Grande, he has been out for most of the night and has done a recce of some roads in the area and he has found a long straight road about three kilometres west of the airbase that he has looked at, and the measurements he has given to us are very promising, the straight part of this road stretches for about four kilometres,' Colonel Thomas said as he was trying to find the road in the Atlas.

'Well, that sounds promising, what do the RAF boys say about it.'

'We are awaiting the Air Chief Marshall and the Director to arrive, and then we will see what they have to say, I do believe that they have someone from four seven squadron with them as well.'

Colonel Cecil walked over to have a look at the map in the Atlas along with Colonel Thomas, but the Atlas was useless, however Colonel Cecil went over to the filing cabinet and returned with a large satellite photograph that he had in the office of the area, he unrolled the photograph and the two men studied it, and with the aid of a magnifying glass they found the road.

'It does not look that wide,' Colonel Cecil remarked.

Colonel Thomas was comparing it to the runway at Rio Grande, 'hmm' you are right it does look rather narrow; we will have to see what the RAF guys think of it when they arrived.'

The two Colonels did not have to wait long

before the RAF officers arrived with the Director, and they squeezed into the office with the two Colonels.

Colonel Thomas had filled the men in on the message received from Rio Grande and they were now all looking at the picture with the narrow strip of road. Colonel Thomas could see a despondent look in the Air Chief Marshall, and along with Group Captain Roberts from Four Seven squadron, and Colonel Thomas was now sure that the plan to land on this road would not be any good.

There was silence in the room for about five minutes and Group Captain Roberts looked up and rubbed his chin and continued to look down at the picture, everyone waited for an answer. 'If your mans figures are correct then there is no reason why we cannot put down on that road, but I cannot emphasise that we will be taking a hell of a risk putting two Hercs on there,'

The Director did not mince his words 'let's get it done,' he said.

Now was a time of frenzy, it was the middle of the night, and everyone involved in an operation was now dragged in out of there beds for the operation, Mikado was now alive and back on the table.

'Excuse me sir but when shall we do it,' Colonel Cecil asked.

'Tomorrow night, we have the men down there sat on their arse, we have the Hercs and crew down there, let's get the job done, the men have trained up ready for this mission, so send them these details, and get our man in Rio Grande to prepare for them to arrive.'

Colonel Cecil went out and over to the radio room and shouted over too one of the signallers 'you, get on the line and inform the ops officer on Ascension that we have a green light for Mikado tomorrow night.'

The signaller sent out the message immediately, there were now other personnel arriving at there posts and most had arrived with a mugs of coffee to help wake themselves up, a coded message was now sent out to all groups in the task force to alert them that Mikado was on green.

'What about the Minister, we should inform him,' someone mentioned in the signals room.

'I suppose I better give him a call,' the Director replied as he turned towards a telephone.

Group Captain Harry Roberts was looking through all the dimensions, he was confident that his squadron could land on that road, 'what vehicles will you be using Len' he asked Colonel Cecil.

'We were looking at four Landrovers and about ten motorcycles,' Len replied.

'Okay, I will have to work out the weights too make sure we can land the Hercs short enough, we can put them down on three thousand feet and take off again at the same length, so we have no problem there. I just need to make sure that we land short and do not need to reverse up or turnaround,'

'We just need the vehicles to hurry the attack up on the airbase, we need to get down the other side of the runway as fast as possible and then to exit the site fast.'

'Okay two Land Rovers, and five bikes in each aircraft, and what about the exit, will you leave the vehicles on site,'

'It may be best too I suppose that way we can get out of there fast,' Len replied.

Harry Roberts was checking all the data, both Hercules would need to refuel a few times each on the way down, this will have to be arranged for the Victor tankers to be ready for them, there was a lot to do and because of the Director's decision to go in tomorrow night there was so little time to do it in. All units involved in the operation were now on full alert and everyone was now planning forward.

The Director returned after his call with the Minister, and it has not gone down to well. 'The man is an idiot,' The Director scowled as he returned to the table, 'I have just told him we are now on standby to go in tomorrow night and he goes into a panic over it all happening too fast and now he would have to wake up the PM in the middle of the bloody night,'

'I thought she did not sleep anyway,' Len replied.

Some of the junior staff in the ops room had got hold of a large sheet of paper and have now drawn up a large diagram of the base from the information received from Chack. They have the runway marked out and the gun emplacements marked out also the hangars, and the barrack building, along with the field kitchen and the position of the gun units on the east end of the airbase on the sea front, also the positions of the aircraft disbursed around the base and the hardened ammunition stores to the north of the base and the underground bunkers near to the barracks, the land around the base is described in detail and also the areas for cover where old building foundations seemed to remain.

There is also a sketch of the roads at the western end of the airbase that head into the country and the possible landing site, and that road is positioned approximately one and a half kilometres south of the base running east to west.

Harry Roberts had one more look at the sketch and said that the pilots will only get one chance to land on that road and that will be it, there is no way they can go around for a second run as they will be picked up, and he has also made it clear that the actual landing may well be picked up on a radar at the base. The pilots could use the radio ariel masts at the base for a reference to make their approach.

The men all went through their various calculations too see if anything would pop up that could halt the operation but so far everything was a high risk but could be done.

CHAPTER FIVE.

Ascension Islands.

Fifty men all elements of "B" Squadron SAS were awoken in the early hours by Squadron Sergeant Major Billy Owen, 'Okay boys stand too, stand too.' He shouted out across building that they have been using as temporary accommodation.

'What's the matter Bill,' someone shouted over as all the lights went on.

'Mikado has been given a green light for tomorrow night, so everyone up and start getting your kit ready, the OC will be along shortly and will explain everything,' Bill shouted over in his loud Welsh voice.

The first ten minutes of being woken up had to sink in, the men were moving around slowly as they took in what had been said, they then moved on to getting there kit ready, today will be a day of going through everything over and over again, checking equipment, getting supplies, drawing weapons and ammunition, if any vehicles are to be taken they will have to double check them all too make sure that everything is in working order and nothing will fail and breakdown when they need it. Some men even grab a quick shower, but all of them start to switch on, they have been practicing this for a while now and even now on the island they have been going out in the two Hercules transport planes around the island and landing at Wideawake airfield and exiting the aircraft already for the unfolding events.

While the SAS men are getting themselves awake, so too are the men of four seven special forces flight, the squadron go beyond all others in making sure that their aircraft can be used to drop in special forces teams in there landing areas, the men will now make sure that the aircraft are up to scratch for the flight and also that pilots know where they will have too land and what dangers they will have to face.

The Hercules C130, s that they use are the standard aircraft, but the crew have done some small modifications to equipment themselves, including sticking instruments that they have scrounged from the Americans to their dashboards over there instruments to make their missions easier.

The pilots in four seven have had their flight helmets modified by a local engineer so that they can change from active infra red goggles to the American passive night vision, as the Argentinians have been picking up the active googles and then zero in on them to target, so all precautions have been made.

The engineers are going over the aircraft and checking everything over ready for the mission everything will be double checked and if anything is suspect it will be changed for a new item.

The pilots are going through everything, all the information that had been sent to Northwood has now been sent to them to go over and over, they now have to plan their route down south, a route that they have made many times in the past few weeks transporting men and goods to the fleet, but today it is different, this time they will push beyond the Falkland Islands and on into the Argentine mainland and this will also be done at extreme low level, they will then have to cross over unknow territory deep into Argentina, enemy ground and with very little information on what to expect when they arrive there.

There are also the refuelling points on the way down, and hopefully on the way back, there aircraft are fitted with extra fuel tanks that they have fitted to the wings, but they will still need extra fuel and with a landing and take off they will burn extra fuel as well.

Northwood has offered a lot of calculations for them on the weights of the men vehicles and fuel, so the calculations are a bit easier for them to work out and will save them valuable time, they will also have to make sure that the pilots have enough sleep, they will take up a back up flight crew to exchange pilots, so they have fresh pilots flying.

When they see the picture that had been faxed to them of where they are expected to land there is general disbelief that they would be dropping down onto a narrow road in the middle of the night in an area that they have never been too or seen before.

A lot of questions start to fly around about everything from roadside furniture too trees and hills, but a lot of the questions were answered for them.

The SAS men who were taking part in the raid were all back inside the large building that they had been using to sleep in. The Commanding Officer Colonel Colin Bradley had just arrived along with the second in command Major Peter Austin, Squadron Sergeant Major Owen is also along with them, and he called out for order, and then he brings the men in closer to listen to the Commanding officer.

'Okay men as you know operation Mikado has been given a green light for tomorrow night, but a lot of things have changed with the mission,' Colonel Bradley turned and then pointed to a small sketch on a blackboard that they had put up, on the boards were a few quick sketched lines, one was the runway, and then the other was a few lines running around it and then a long line just below going away from the airbase. 'Okay men, this is just a rough sketch, you will be given more details as we go on,' Bradley used his swagger stick to point over towards the runway, this is the target area, now we have intel that has picked out a number of gun emplacements, there are two here at the west end of the runway, then we move here halfway up the runway where another gun is situated here, and then there are about three up here on the eastern end on the sea front,' Bradley looks around too make sure everyone is paying attention, and then we have another large gun battery here to the south. We then have a hangar where we believe there are four Exocet missiles inside, there is a small barrack building here where indications show that there are men at about Company strength, but these are conscripts.' Bradley looked around again and paused for a moment he watched as the senior and junior NCO, s wrote down notes in their notebooks he then continued to show the positions of the aircraft that they believe were at the base and describe how the Super Etendards were actually hidden in the streets next to the airbase.

'Now the shitty stuff,' Bradley said and then continued 'We cannot land at the base like we had planned, so we have an alternative landing area, here about five or six kilometres away on a dirt road west of the base. We will land here and then advance to the base as fast as possible, our target will be to take out the machine guns first on the runway and the south side of the base, we will then move as carefully as we can sending a troop down the runway to attack the four Etendards and then plant ready made explosives on them, at the same time a troop will plant explosives on the four Skyhawk aircraft and another troop will attack the hangar and plant explosives on the missiles.'

Bradley paused for a moment and then continued, 'this is just a brief plan at the moment we will give you full orders shortly, but we will then withdraw and as we do so we will plant explosives at this underground bunker. We will then haul our arse out of there back to the aircraft as fast as we can, now the real bad news is that somewhere around this airbase are what we believe to be a battalion of Marines and also a group of Argentine special forces, so we need to hit the place and run if we can and get out before they realise what had hit them.'

The room remained quite while Colonel Bradley looked around, there were a few brief exchanges of words within the men when he mentioned the fact that there were Marines and special forces based there but as he hoped this did not worry his men that he had gathered in front of him.

Major Austin moved forward to say a few words, 'Well men get yourself into your troop and we will go through the plans with you, and each group will have their targets at the base, are there any questions,'

'What happens if the Hercs get hit on the ground,' someone at the rear shouted.

'Good question, you will all have an emergency pack with rations, the border with Chile is about thirty miles away so we will all head for the border and take our chances there.'

'Are we using silenced weapons in the attack.' Another man shouted.

'That has to be decided, we may well use them in the initial element of the attack but if we are counter attacked then we will use everything we have got and that will include the loud stuff.'

Major Austin paused and looked around the room 'any more questions,' he called but there were none at this stage.

For this mission, the men were split into four troops of ten men, and each troop will be led by an officer.

Alpha troop will be commanded by Major John Billings, a well liked officer a quite man in his late thirties tall thin and intelligent black hair thinning on top.

Bravo troop will be commanded by Captain Khan Rasheed, who joined the Regiment from the Parachute Regiment, a tall man born in the UK to Indian parents who settled in the UK many years ago, he would never ask his men to do anything that he could not do himself, however he is a man who can do almost anything, and he tends to push his men hard.

Charlie troop will be commanded by Captain Jeremy Hastings, he has not long been in the Regiment, and had come over from the Royal Green Jackets.

Delta troop will be commanded by Captain

Len Smith, a more mature officer who has risen through the lower ranks, and he is very respected because his head is full of knowledge from years of experience, Smith is in his late forties but as fit as the youngest man he is a thick built man with a grey balding head.

Headquarters troop commanded by Colonel Bradley.

The men return to their troop, each troop, will be issued a task to carry out at the base when they get there.

Alpha troop will be tasked to be the first ones in, there targets will be the two gun groups on the western end of the runway, they will also advance and eliminate the gun that is situated halfway down the runway on the southern side.

Bravo troop have been assigned to advance down the runway once the gun groups have been eliminated. The ten men will use motorcycles to advance down the runway, there target will be the four super Etendard aircraft parked at the eastern end. They will also if possible and subject to being available target the four Dagger aircraft at that end of the runway as they may well be parked on the north side off the runway opposite the Etendard Jets.

Alpha troop at this stage will move forward to the taxiway that runs over to the apron and hangar where the Skyhawk Jets are parked and the hangar where the Exocet missiles are being stored, Alpha troop will give cover to both the returning

Bravo troop and also cover for Charlie and Delta troop.

Delta troop will approach and attack the gun emplacement on the southern side of the airbase that is positioned near to the underground bunker and the billets.

Charlie troop will go around them too the south and then come back along the drive and then advance too the hangar where they will plant explosives onto the Exocet missiles that are stored within, they will also move together with Delta troop and plant explosives on the four Skyhawk aircraft.

All troops will then cover and then withdraw to the road in the west and make their way back too the C130s that will be ready to roll, all vehicles will be left behind and either left as is or will be fitted with explosives to destroy them.

This is the plan so far; All troops will be led into the airbase by Chack who will meet the aircraft when they land and guide all troops in towards their target.

Headquarters troop will control all groups on radio, and they will also provide sentries to the west and east of the landing zone and will be in charge of the vehicles.

The plan so far has not been any different to that of the original plan where the two Hercules would land at the airbase on the runway, and then the SAS troops would launch the attack, the only difference now is that they now know of all the gun emplacements in the area and also the troop numbers that are stationed there.

A new decision has now been made that two weapons will be carried, they will carry the CAR 15 rifle as they always do but will also carry the Heckler and Koch MP5SD silenced 9mm sub machine gun, these will be used on the initial attacks to remain as discreet as possible, and for as long as possible, not only are these weapons silent but they also have the ability to hide some of the muzzle flash from each round that is fired, so with luck they will not be seen or heard on the airbase. They will also carry their CAR 15 rifles with 5.56 mm rounds for self defence if they are discovered by the Argentine forces and they need to put down a substantial fire power in a fire fight.

They will take three Landrovers in each C130, each Landrover will be equipped with two 7.62 general purpose machine guns that will be fitted to a sustained fire fixing on the actual vehicle, these weapons will bring down sustained machine gun fire in support of the troops on the ground.

The men will also carry M72 light anti tank rocket launchers and also hand held 203 grenade launchers, as well as grenades, smoke grenades and flashbangs.

After spending a number of hours during the daytime going over each scenario it was decided that the men would be ready, but the niggle in the background is that they needed more time to work out there plans for this mission.

In the meantime, the RAF 47 squadron had worked out their route as best they could on the information that they had, they will fly south at high altitude and make two refuels on the way down, they would turn and head west just south of the Falkland Islands, under cover of darkness and they would then at a safe distance from the mainland drop down to just above sea level for there approach towards the Argentine mainland.

They are aiming to hit land just north of a small town called Cabo San Pablo, and then head east inland until they reach Lago Chepelmuth, a large lake that is just north of another lake lago Yehuin.

They will then turn and head north east towards the border, and after eighty kilometres they will turn east and then head towards the road that they will use for a landing, they have the references sent to them from the Magellan GPS that Chack is carrying with him so they can make their adjustments.

Chack will have too be at the side of the road and signal to them as they approach and give them an indication of where the rad starts to go straight for the landing. The two Hercules will be flying as low as they dare on the way in, the pilots prey that there are no overhead cables anywhere that could not be seen on the surveillance photographs.

The pilots will now grab some sleep, they have a long flight in front of them later today. While they are sleeping the engineers are busy preparing the aircraft and also loading the vehicles, the first problem was that Northwood stated two Landrovers for each Hercules and now three per aircraft have turned up, so now new fuel calculations will have too be looked at because of the extra weight.

The Hercules are now fuelled up ready and everything is double checked, oil levels checked engines checked and hydraulics are checked. The C130 is considered a robust aircraft and not much goes wrong with them so the engineers are happy that these aircraft will go in and do the job.

The worry is that they are big and fat and not very fast, so they are at high risk when they are flying low into Argentina.

The SAS squadron are now busy going through the routine of checking and double checking all weapons and cleaning them and test firing them at the small range they have, they then go through all their kit to make sure that they have everything that have will need including there Browning hi power 9 mm side arm.

There kit will not be heavy, they will carry a lightweight escape and evasion kit just in case they have to make a run towards the border, but other than that they will just concentrate on the kit needed for the attack.

Each man has been warned that if caught they could be jailed or even executed for being spies as the two Governments have not declared war against each other, they will not be covered by the Geneva convention.

Everyone has one last job to do and that is to make out there last will and testament just in case. One more chat from the CO and maybe a few words from the Padre and a prayer, his door will be open for all to come and see him.

The banter kicks off amongst the men as well, a last minute piss take makes the day seem normal and relieves the pressure that the oncoming mission will bring with it.

Mobility, are checking the vehicles, again they will make sure that everything will start on the key, any doubt then it will not be loaded up, all oil levels are checked, and all fluid levels are checked as well, the GPMG machines guns are cleaned, and test fired and made ready before they are made safe and then mounted to the vehicles. The vehicles are then all fuelled up ready for the mission, once ready they are taken down to the two Hercules that are on the apron ready to go. The men and vehicles will be divided between the two aircraft, it was decided to use the two aircraft just in case one failed at least they had the option of getting half the men there and maybe successfully carrying out the raid, also if one Hercules does get damaged on the mission, they will have the other one to bring them all out and back home.

The RAF will take a small group of men with them as well in each aircraft to assist in the fast unloading of vehicles and also a couple of engineers just in case they are needed if there was a small breakdown of any part on the aircraft.

The SAS officers were deep in planning, a map was described to them over the phone that they had drawn up in Northwood, with the use of a white bed sheet and a felt tip pen the officers had now managed to make out a map of the airbase from the information that was given too them from Northwood, this large scale map has now made there planning a little easier.

Each known anti aircraft gun position has been marked out the guns are well covered with a berm built around them to protect them, these will have to be dealt with before they move onto the targets, and also, if possible, the two bunkers that, if possible, they can attack, but the word back from Northwood was, to concentrate on the Super Etendard and the Exocet missiles, these are the priority at the moment as the Exocet missiles are the biggest threat to the fleet.

In the meantime, back in Argentina the sun had come up on another southern hemispheres winter day, so far today there had been some heavy showers blowing through making life uncomfortable for Chack who was now busy checking over the road in daylight, there is a big difference, between looking at the road at night, and then going back to it during the day and looking at it again.

Now it has rained onto the road it looks so much different and Chack now feels more anxious about the grip on the road, the last thing he would want is the two aircraft landing and then skidding off the road into the ditches at the side.

Chack has been busy walking along the road and marking off every, one hundred feet. The Hercs will need three thousand feet to land and take off again over the same difference, that is no problem, what Chack was now doing was working out to make sure that they would have the harder ground each side for the Land Rovers to drive over when the exit the rear of the aircraft, he also needed to make sure that the first aircraft will leave enough room for the second one to come in and land behind it.

There was still so much to do, this area was notorious for rubbish blowing around in the constant winds, so Chack had to make sure that all pieces of plastic or any other lose items would not be blown up and into one of the engines. And finally, he had to make sure that there were no other pieces of roadside furniture on the side of the road that he may have missed.

Once he had checked it all out and then double checked it all out, he then set up a stick in one of the surrounding fields with a piece of cloth on it so that he could watch the wind direction for the aircraft.

And finally, one more check and that was to make sure that his torch worked as he will have to use that to wave at the aircraft to bring them in. Then as soon as they are down, he will have a three thousand feet dash to guide them to the best spot for the unload.

Everything that he could think off he has done over and over a number of times. Now is the time when as Chack would say too himself 'shit or bust.'

CHAPTER SIX.

Northwood.

The sun was starting to go down at Northwood and the SAS ops room was now settling down as the mission had started.

'I just hope to God this does not go the same way as operation Eagle Claw did for the Yanks,' Len Cedric said to Bill Thomas, the two Colonels were preparing for a long night, the flight alone was a daring one, with a number of air to air refuelling's on the way there and back adding too the dangers of the mission.

Operation Eagle Claw was an attempted rescue mission authorised by President Jimmy Carter in 1980. The operation by the United States Delta force was one of there first missions and was carried out to rescue fifty-two hostages that had been held captive at the United States Embassy in Tehran, Iran.

The mission faced many obstacles during its operation phase and had to be abandoned, Eight helicopters were sent into the area of the first stage called desert one but only five arrived there in an operational condition, because of this the operation was called off, but one of the helicopters that had taken off to leave the area then struck a Air Force transport aircraft that had been carrying Jet fuel for the mission resulting in a explosion and fire that left eight service men killed

The only communication Northwood would have would be via satellite phone links so any news would have to be passed around before it reached Northwood.

The Director and the Minister were in the conference room in talks, even now there was the fear that the plug could be pulled on the mission, maybe it was a bit too daring, if British lives are lost on the mainland of Argentina, then there could be a backlash from the public.

But the Director was confident that his men would do the job even if they lost the two Hercules it was considered a cost to pay to save any more ships from being hit. The Minister was in a verbal brawl earlier in the day when one of the Admirals launched a scathing attack into him as to why they were still in talks with selling the carriers that the navy had.

'And do you realise that if we still had the Ark Royal with Phantoms and Buccaneers this war would have been wound up by now,' the Admiral shouted across the room. The Minister reeled from this and had no answer, cuts look good on paper but when they are faced with what they are faced with now then they can see how foolish their decisions are, even the Harrier was, at this time being written into history as 'just a plane that can do tricks at an air show, like tip its head and bow to the people,' all this was thrown at the minister as the Harriers start to mark up there success rates so far in the war.

'I hear the Prime Minister will be up all night waiting for news,' Bill Thomas said to Len Cedric as they drank another coffee that seemed to be an endless item in the room.

'So, I hear, let us just hope we can pull this all off.'

As the men in Northwood waited in almost silence the men of the SAS had now boarded the two Hercules C130 aircraft, as usual there was the normal banter as the men walked onto the aircraft, even a football appeared onboard the first Hercules, and that was quickly bounced around the rear cargo bay.

Once the men had sat down, they then secured the football and then started to secure themselves and their kit. With the Land Rovers and the motorcycles now secured inside the Hercules, there was not much room left for the men and their equipment on each side.

The seating onboard was nothing more than a deck chair style of seat, it was a canvas foldable seat and now this is the only comfort that the men will get on the very long journey down south. Each man had also made sure that he had emptied his bladder and his bowel before the trip as there were no conveniences onboard only a large plastic container that had been secured up at one end.

The flight will take around twelve hours or longer for the distance that the two aircraft will be flying as they make there way south of the Falkland Islands and then head towards the west into Argentina.

The men are leaving the heat and humidity of Ascension Island, and soon they will feel a sharp shock when they arrive at there destination in Argentina. As they all settle down inside the two aircraft now know from their call sign as Omen One and Two, they now plug their ears with the sponge type ear defenders that they use on the rifle ranges, to deaden out the drone from the engines on the Hercules.

The two aircraft now start to move, it is still light here as they roll along the runway to there take off position. All last minute checks take place all pressures are checked to see if they are okay and then the Omen One starts its take off, once it rolled down the runway it is then followed by Omen Two, that now rolled along behind it. The two aircraft then turn and head south towards there first rendezvous with the first Victor tanker that will be waiting for them to refuel.

The SAS men have now settled down for the fight, a couple of them have now even inched over and climbed into the land Rovers to take advantage of the better seating that the Land Rovers will provide them with. And the rest of the men are now taking the advantage of getting some sleep while they can, knowing full well that this could be a short successful mission or a long one complete with an escape and evasion run for the next few days attached to it.

Colonel Bradley has now moved over to the bonnet of one of the Land Rovers onboard Omen one, he has now unrolled the bed sheet map that they had made up and was now going through the options and looking for anything that could prevent the mission from being a success, things could go easily wrong he thought as he was now joined by Major Austin and now both men were leaning against the bonnet of the Land Rover and over the map together discussing the mission.

The first refuel point had been reached and it was now dark as the Hercules descended to meet the Victor, the refuelling probe that stuck out over the flight cabin was carefully aimed at the basket and after one gentle attempt and careful use of a torch, Omen One had attached itself to the fuel hose and was now filling up with fuel.

After Omen One had refuelled it was now the turn of Omen Two who after several attempts finally connected up to take on board some fuel.

The two Hercules now refuelled returned to there cruising hight and continued south towards there next refuelling point.

Northwood were now receiving dispatches of information, first about a successful take off of both aircraft and then they received another message to say that both aircraft had taken there first refuel. It was a full relief to everyone, that so far that everything had gone to plan.

There was suddenly a rumour floating around Northwood that there could be a peace plan on the table, there were many raised eyebrows at the news floating in, so far no one knew of the source of the rumour. Colonel Thomas phoned the Director and asked him 'Sorry Sir but we have just picked up on a rumour of a possible peace deal being negotiated.'

'A peace deal, this is news to me, I will have to dig around, how is the mission going so far,' the Director answered.

'So far so good, we have had no problems,' Colonel Thomas answered.

'Good, well keep the mission running no matter what we hear at the moment, I will get onto the Minister and find out what is going on.'

Colonel Thomas placed the phone down and walked over to Len Cedric, 'The Director has not heard anything about any peace deal, but he is going to ask the minister now just in case, but he said keep the mission n track.'

'Okay, everything is fine at the moment the last thing we want is to call it all off over some talks that may well fall apart,' Cedric replied.

*

Chack was now holding up in a small ditch away from the road, it has started to go dark, and he has decided to pull out his small gas stove and get a brew going, he has not had a hot drink since the night before, he checked his water bottles and still had enough water on him for now, but he had not taken that much in during the day.

He had opened up a tin of chicken curry as well and had decided to have that cold, the sooner the stove was turned off the better. There had been a few cars up and down along here during the daytime, and Chack was a bit concerned about the traffic, he had been alerted that the birds were in the air and worked out that they would be there around midnight. That would be a long way off as yet. Chack sat there drinking his coffee and eating the cold curry and wondered what the Argentine field Kitchen had on the menu tonight.

*

At the Rio Grande airbase the time had come to change gun crew for the night shift that took over during the night. The truck trundled around to the western end of the runway and again with all the banter and the throwing of items the two gun crews were exchanged. The truck then went along the runway to change the other gun crew on the northern edge of the runway and then onwards to the Ammunition dump in the north to change the guards down around the hardened bunkers, before returning the men to the barracks.

*

As Chack had found out over the past few days although the officers think that it was a possibility that the base would be attacked by British special forces, the conscript soldiers thought that this was unlikely, and most settled in next to there guns and then went to sleep. If there was aircraft coming in with special forces, they would hear it.

*

On the weeks leading up to the mission the SAS men had done some training to prepare just in case they were sent into Rio Grande. The preparations including a number of Hercules flights into a number of coastal air bases, it was then that they found just how easy it would be for the Argentinians to track a Hercules heading into the base.

Also, during the training, they were visited by a Royal Marine Commando, the Commando was a typical Marine, short thickset man with an angular chin and a flat nose and short curly hair.

This Marine however was a warrant officer, Sergeant Major Barry Bufton, who had actually trained with the Argentine Marines and also elements of the special forces Buzos Tacticos.

Bufton was one of those mean type of men who never seemed to smile much, he was visiting the Regiment too inform the men jut what the Argentine Marines and special forces were like.

He stood in front of the men in the conference hall and started off with his introduction to who he was and what he had done.

'Okay Gentlemen, you make think that you are the best men on the planet, but I have worked with these forces over the years and have got to know what they are like,' he said as he opened up to the men, he also had pictures of the commandos in training on the wall behind him. 'These guys are no push over; they are not conscripts and they are not useless in what they do, they like you are highly trained, they are the best of the best.' Bufton paused as he looked on at the men.

'I know you lot may be regarded as the best but believe me these guys are just as good, and if you have to fight them then you will have a fight on your hands.' Bufton went through how they had trained, and just how tough they were, and the men in the room were impressed by what he had to say about them.

Bufton finished off his talk with the following, 'Okay, my advice to you is to try and avoid all contact with them, hit the target and get out fast, you do not have to fight them, and then you will all live another day.'

The men were all taken back by the revelation of the Argentinians, and to Sergeant Major Bufton's pleasure, he spent another two hours talking with the men who all wanted to know everything about them. The more you know about your enemy, the better you can fight him. Most of the SAS men would not hold back on a fight with the Argentine marines and special forces if it came to it, but they were there to do a hit and run mission and leave in one piece.

*

The two Hercules, Omen One and Two, were now at their second refuelling point, and this was also there last one before heading inland towards there target. Again, Omen One was first to take on the fuel and this time it took a few attempts to engage with the basket as they were now in a more turbulent air stream and the air had also started to get worse the further south they travelled.

Again, Omen One had filled up with its fuel and then broke loose and held off while Omen Two moved forward to refuel, again Omen Two had a few problems but finally engaged the basket and refuelled.

The two Hercules aircraft now headed a further distance south, and then started a slow turn to head a distance south of the Falkland Islands and then west in towards the Argentine mainland.

Once they were one hundred miles south of the Falklands they headed west, for 250 miles at altitude, they then descended down to low level for the run in towards Argentina.

The SAS men were all comfortable as they could be in the seats in the cargo bay of the Hercules, but they now became aware that the aircraft were both heading down into a dive towards low altitude, the two aircraft were now buffeting around in the turbulence that was to be found at the lower levels, everything was starting to shake about and it was getting even worse as they dropped even lower, to a lower altitude that was only around thirty feet above the sea, and if possible the pilots would go even lower to try and evade any radar.

There was even more turbulence being thrown from the ocean as the two aircraft raced across the sky towards the main land, things seemed to be getting bad when a few of the men opened up their sick bags. The Colonel was assured that this part of the flight would only take about forty minutes, and then they would be back over land and things would get better.

The Land Rovers now seemed to be moving around, but a quick check by the RAF loaders showed that they were all still secured. The SAS men who were all now awake all looked around the cabin as pieces of lose straps and wires were all swinging around, the football that someone had carried on was now rolling around with a life of its own and every now and then the Hercules would give a violent jolt to one side as if it had hit something.

The pilot and co pilot were now wearing night vision googles as they approached the mainland, they were seeking lights on the horizon that would indicate Faro Cabo San Pablo, but so far, they could not see anything, they were beginning to think that their calculations were off, and a check with the stars was now impossible as they were now beneath heavy clouded skies.

The two Hercules continued there run in towards the mainland when they suddenly see some lights, for a moment they thought that it was the lights of the town only to discover that they were passing a ship at low level, they hoped as they were flying low and dark that the ship would not have noticed the aircraft as they flew by.

The pilot would have to make the Colonel aware of the ship, they all knew there was a risk that they could be seen but this was a little bit early in the mission and they were concerned that the ship may send a message about the encounter that could warn the Argentine military.

The two Hercules carried on and then finally they could see lights ahead. Too the left they could see what looked almost like the white cliffs of Dover and they were now heading at low level between these two points.

*

Northwood had now received the signal that Omen One and Two had completed there second and final refuel before heading into the mainland, the room was tense as everyone was now trying to guess where the two aircraft currently were positioned in the south Atlantic south of the Falkland Islands.

'They will be at low level now,' Colonel Cedric said in a bid to break the silence.

'It will be up to the pilots now to get them into position, let us hope everything goes to plan,' Colonel Thomas replied.

'Now I know how they all felt on the Dam busters raid,' Colonel Cedric commented.

'Anything more on that peace deal we heard about earlier,' Cedric asked.

'I think, it was all just some talk in the press,'

Thomas replied.

'The papers will print any junk now days.'

The two Hercules crossed over the coastline and into Argentina, there was some high ground to their left, and the right, and that would shield them for now, but all pilots were now concentrating on the land in front of them and could see some small hills that they would have to navigate around, there was also now chatter between the two aircraft Omen One was now chatting too Omen Two informing them of any hills or land marks in front.

The two aircraft flew on a little slower now to give them more of a chance to see and avoid anything that may crop up. The rear of the aircraft was not much better, there was a lot of bouncing around from the low level flying and every now and then there would be a loud bang as the Hercules jumped around up and down and from side to side in a turbulent airflow.

The pilots were now even more busy, both were watching out for obstacles on the horizon, anything from trees to power lines to chimney stacks and buildings.

The ground was not dead flat as they first expected, there were rises in the ground taking the ground up and down, the pilots now had to keep their aircraft as low as possible and follow this terrain.

This part of the flight was better than they had hoped at least they were now confident that they would stay below any long range radar.

After about thirty minutes they came towards the lakes that they were looking for, straight ahead and dead on target in front of them, this would be there turning point.

Too the south of them hills started to come up like small mountains where the land had now changed to a more mountainous region, but as they looked north the land seemed flatter.

The two Hercules thundered low over the lakes and then went through a small valley, once they were at the end of the valley, they checked there co ordinates and then turned sharp to starboard and then headed towards the north.

They found that there were a few low valleys and low hills along the route so they could in fact keep lower, again they were looking for any advantage to keep the aircraft out of radar. There target was the Rio Grande river that will run from west to east towards the city of Rio Grande they knew that after this they would have to use the Magellan co ordinates that they were supplied with to turn and head west towards the road that they would use for the landing.

They slowed up a touch, both Hercules pilots form the two Hercules were keeping in constant contact advising each other of any movements they are going to make as they keep in a close formation, one behind the other.

It was now 23,38 as the two Hercules reached there next turning point and could see a point just in front with a few raised areas, small hills that would give them some cover as they made there turn to starboard again and then head east. At Laguna las Tres Marias, a small lake, the two Hercules turned, and were now headed east towards there landing strip on the road that had been picked out.

The pilots could see a change in the terrain below them as they headed east, now they will have to keep as low as they can as they travelled the last sixteen kilometres to the landing site they now slowed up ready, they were now looking out for a torch light that will be waved in front of them, it was almost like looking for a needle in a haystack, meanwhile Omen Two had slowed up to create a small gap between the two aircraft, there was only going to be one attempt at landing and if it goes wrong and they have to abort then the mission would be scrubbed and both aircraft will have to head back home.

CHAPTER SEVEN.

23.55 Estancia Maria Behety, Argentina.

At the small hamlet of Estancia Maria Behety where they have a vast sheep farm all across the area they were suddenly awaken to an almighty roar of engines as Omen One went almost overhead, one of the men in the small village was outside at the time just checking on his own stock of animals before he retired to his bed, he saw a dark shadow heading towards him and then so low he feared that it would take the roof away from his house, he cried out to his wife as he watched Omen One head east then as he was just getting over the shock of seeing Omen One Omen Two came over on a identical route and again low enough to remove the roof.

His initial shock turned into excitement, and now some of his neighbours have come out of their houses to join him and to investigate the sudden noise, and now they have all concluded that the aircraft would be from the base at Rio Grande taking part in practice for the Malvinas war, or even returning from the Islands.

*

Chack had set up on the side of the road, apart from a car heading west at about 22.30 nothing else had come through all evening, it was now cold, and Chack was looking to make sure that there was no ice forming anywhere.

The estimated time of arrival for Omen One and Two was at around midnight, Chack checked his watch, and it was two minutes to go, he could then hear a rumble in the distance, Chack, got up and ran to the side of the road, his initial thoughts were that a truck was coming along, but there were no lights from any vehicle heading in, and now he knew it had to be the Hercules aircraft.

Chack switched on his torch and then waved it from left and too the right in a large swinging arc, as he looked on, he could now see a large object like a huge shadow heading directly towards him just coming over the top of a small rise in the road to the east, he kept on waving his torch and could now see the huge Hercules almost touching the ground as it hurtled towards him. As the Hercules reached Chack, he dived down flat on to the ground, and the huge Hercules went over the top as it touched down onto the road. And as soon as it passed over him, Chack, was back on his feet again, and waving again as Omen two came in following Omen One, and again touching down onto the road, both Hercules had landed without any lights the only light that could be seen, was the tail light from Omen One that was illuminated for a few minutes to give Omen Two, and idea where Omen

One was on the ground.

The Pilots onboard the Omen flight were now at a very low level, they had just seen a small village below them as they went overhead at low level and the thought of the poor people in those house that would have probably fallen out of there beds with the sound of the Hercules flying over, first Omen one and then followed by Omen two.

The pilots had now extended their flaps and were reducing the speed of there aircraft all the time they were in communication with each aircraft advising the other what movements and speed they were doing so each crew knew what the other one was doing. They now lowered the wheels of the Hercules not only to make the landing but to make sure that they had full undercarriage and also the wheels down would help with slowing the aircraft down.

They were now busy looking for a torch signal up ahead to guide them to the road where it became straight, this would be for them to drop down onto the road. They could just about see a light waving in front of them and with the use of only night vision googles they will land on the road next to the light.

Omen One informed Omen Two of the light and then Omen One dropped down to the road for the landing 'Shit or bust,' was said at this point as the aircraft with approximately sixty nine thousand kilos of weight come down onto the road. The Hercules came down with a bump, but this became a nice smooth landing, although there was a lot of noise now entering the aircraft from the uneven road surface, as it thundered towards a halt.

Omen One was now safely down and would have to make sure that it gave enough room at its rear, for Omen Two to land behind it, so the pilots made sure that they did not come to a complete halt but moved forward to give Omen Two some room to pull up.

Consideration was given to Omen Two as it would also come through the turbulent air created by Omen one as it touched down behind it.

Omen Two was now on approach the pilots could see the torch being waved at them as they dropped down, but they came down a little bit harder onto the ground behind Omen One. The pilots managed to slow there aircraft and to pull up, and with the distance that Omen One had left they came in with about twenty feet to spare from their nose to Omen Ones tail.

As the two aircraft came into land the SAS men were being battered from side to side as the Hercules was buffeted by side winds and up drafts from below, the red lights in the cabin were now on and each man was now preparing for the landing, even though they have been on a Hercules before the noises that they hear from final adjustments put the men on edge as the aircraft starts to adjust for landing, and then the sound of the wheels going down and the thuds when the wheels lock into place, all these things make all the men extra anxious as so many things could go wrong during a landing.

The men then wait for the big aircraft too hit the ground for the landing, in Omen One that came as a smooth landing, but they could feel the Hercules bumping around and following ruts in the ground as it ran along the road, then they could feel the force from the brakes as the big aircraft started to shed its speed and slow down towards a halt.

Onboard Omen Two there journey in was a lot more uncomfortable, as Omen Two had followed Omen One, into the landing it was flying into the turbulent air that had been whisked up by Omen One, on top of all this there was also the wind factor, and the up drafts to contend with, as they made there approach, the men were, as they were in the lead aircraft, feeling anxious as they came into land and again they sat and listened to all the noises with a heightened sensitivity for each creak and each noise of the aircraft being adjusted for the landing.

Then the wheels went down and locked into position and then they came in hard with a bit of a bounce as they hit the road surface and landed. And then just like Omen One, Omen Two had to apply the brakes to come to a halt but this time with the danger that Omen One was already down in front of them, and already at a halt, there was no way they could abort and do a go around, this was one landing, and one landing only, but with the skill of the pilots they were down, and they came to a halt twenty feet behind Omen One.

Both Hercules were down and now Chack, had a three thousand feet run to catch up and guide the aircraft to a safe spot where the vehicles could be unloaded. The rear loading doors on both aircraft were now open and the interior lights were on illuminating the Land Rovers, and men who were now all up and moving around in preparation. Two men from Omen Two had now exited the rear of the aircraft, and with weapons at the ready, and a bergen on there back they were now out of the aircraft and running a distance west to set up a road block just in case anyone comes along the road.

Meanwhile a Land Rover was unsecured from Omen one and was already down the ramp and was now going around the aircraft and heading all the way down the road to the end of the straight, to prevent any vehicle from coming up the road from the east.

As the two sentry positions had been secured all the Land Rovers and motorcycles were now unloaded from the aircraft, and Colonel Bradley was out and looking around for Chack, who at the time was just checking everything with some of the men before the Colonel grabbed him to pull to one side and just him to quickly go over things on the map they had made.

Chack was now looking at the map with the Colonel and explaining each position too him, Colonel Bradley had to make the decisions on what targets to take out at the base, the mission only required the Exocet and the Etendard jets, but the more damage they can do the better. While they were going through everything on the map, Major Austin joined them to take a look, and the RAF crew were also now out checking the two aircraft over to make sure they were okay for the take off.

All the men were now ready to go and Chack would go up front, he had explained to Colonel Bradley how the land was boggy at the west end of the airbase and would be difficult for the Land Rover to gain any grip, so the land Rovers would carry the men up to the end of the road then would have to be hidden while the men entered on foot towards their targets,

The motorcycles could be pushed through the outer fence and then used to run down the runway once the three gun positions had been cleared along the runway, some confusion was around as they all thought that going into the base by vehicle would be easy, but the nature of the land meant that a lot of it would have to be done on foot.

Colonel Bradley and Major Austin were now happy, and they both wanted to move on, it was now 00,08 and no one seemed to have noticed their arrival as no forces had been sent out up to now.

'Gather the men into their troops,' Major Austin said over the comms, and everyone headed too their Land Rovers and took up their positions, the convoy was now ready to move and with Chack, now in the front Land Rover, the Land Rovers and motorcycles now headed along the road towards the base.

Meanwhile the pilots were now all together planning there exit, they knew as soon as they lifted off then they would be picked up on enemy radar, and the fear was that there may be other anti aircraft guns about with a Radar fitted. As they worked out their plans the aircraft engineers were busy checking the two aircraft over to make sure they would be able to take off and make their way back home.

There are so many things to do but the main fear will be getting caught by gunfire or fighter aircraft that may well be sent up, the pilots had made their concerns be known to Colonel Bradley who will now look at the situation at the base and make a decision on what aircraft to attack on the ground when they get there.

The Land Rovers now reach the end of the straight and go past the Land Rover that is on sentry duty at the end of the road. They then pull into the narrow road that Chack looked at earlier in the day, and the decision has been made to park up the Land Rovers here and then go in on foot towards the air base, as it is just under three kilometres along the road from here, the Colonel thinks that with a bit of a quick walk it would loosen up the men's legs after the long flight, and get their circulation going, the road from here is like everything else around here and that is flat. The motorcycle will follow but will have to keep their revs down as they do not want to make any noise and give away their approach towards the base.

As the men move forward along the road towards the base, they all seem to be getting into the swing, the Colonel was correct in this thoughts as the walk has done them good and loosened them all up. As the base comes into sight the Colonel now gets a better view of things, and he can now see for himself how the land is set up towards the runway and buildings.

'Bugger, there is not much cover out there,' the Colonel said as he stopped and pulled Major Austin to one side, the men take a defensive position as the two officers take any cover they can find, while they look on towards the base.

'There is no way we can get any vehicles in there,' Major Austin commented as they looked on. Colonel Bradley looked at his watch 00.28, we are wasting time here, we need to push on,' he said as he looked around.

Colonel Bradley looked around for Captain Rasheed and summoned him over, 'now Khan, can you take your men on foot, and then sneak around the south side of the runway, and then take the gun emplacement out that they have halfway down on the south.'

'Yes Colonel,' Rasheed replied.

Okay then, when you move along, and at the same time, I will get Major Billings to take out the two gun Emplacements at the west end of the runway, just in front of us, he can do it along with Captain Hastings. So, it will be Bravo team down there and Alpha and Charlie take out the two guns here and we will move onto the next position afterwards.'

The officers all agreed the plan and moved forward, each troop will be ten men strong, and all will use there suppressed MP5SD weapons to take the targets in silence, and they all have their comms system linked into each other so they will all move into their position before they strike.

Bravo troop will have the longest movement to make, and they will also head in towards the target along with Chack, who will be taking all the men into the area, by a path that he had found that avoids most of the bog.

Chack will take the men through the outer fence, they find that outer fence to the airbase was also low and has been unmaintained, so it will be easy to climb over one at a time. Then one team will move forward to the fence and then they will set up a position to provide cover for the teams that will go over the fence. Once these men have climbed over the fence and moved forward, they will then find suitable positions to give cover for the rear covering team to then move forward over the fence and join them in the open area.

There are now thirty SAS men inside the outer perimeter of the airbase, Chack now moves past the SAS men towards the front, and then he will lead them on towards a safe area where he himself had been laid up watching the air base for the past few days.

As he had explained to them all, the lights on the runway only get turned on, when they know an aircraft is in coming, or if they have aircraft ready to take off, so the runway and surrounding area is now in total darkness except for the lights of any buildings around the area.

Chack, now leads the line of SAS men up towards the left hand corner of the inner perimeter fence so that they can then enter the main part of the base along the runway, and there in front of them was a perimeter road that went around the outside of the runway and was also used for the occasional vehicle patrol, when the Argentine army ever had one.

Chack now led them to the fence that he had cut a hole into and then showed the SAS men where the two gun emplacements were positioned at the western end of the runway.

The officers looked on and now could see for themselves the shadow of the gun emplacements in the darkness, and they could also see that they would be easy to sneak up onto. The men each slid under the fence ad crawled to the edge of the runway, Captain Rasheed had now gathered Bravo troop ready to move along the southern edge of the perimeter road towards the gun position that was positioned halfway down the runway.

In the meantime, while Bravo troop moved

in towards their assault launch position, Charlie and Alpha troop began to slowly move around the rear of the two gun emplacements on end of the runway at the western edge, all the time the men kept down low crawling along on their bellies towards there targets.

Both Alpha and Charlie troop, were now in position, and to there delight they could actually hear snoring coming from the gun emplacements, that were in front of them.

The two groups now awaited Bravo troop to move into position ready for there attack and everyone was now ready to move. Rasheed came over the comms *'Bravo in position and ready.'*

'Alpha ready.'

'Charlie ready.'

'After three, two, one. go, go, go.' Major Billings commanded, and at that Alpha and Charlie troop moved quickly forward in the darkness with complete silence they moved keeping as low as possible, and then with the silenced MP5SD sub machine guns, they cut down the four men in each gun emplacement, there was not a sound form any of them, as they were cut down by total surprise.

At the same time Captain Rasheed along with Bravo troop moved forward on the two man gun position, again they caught the two men in the gun position fast asleep as they moved slowly through them, the only sound was the silenced "phttt" sound from the weapons and one ricochet that hit the ground and spun through the air with a sound that reminded everyone of the western movies they used to watch as kids at the Cinema. Everything was down in complete silence and the men waited for a while just to make sure that they had not disturbed anyone.

All three of the troops had now held ready to move forward to the next target and await further instructions from Colonel Bradley.

Alpha and Bravo troop were now ordered to move down to the east end of the runway, there targets are the four Etendard aircraft and also the four Dagger aircraft.

Captain Rasheed will lead the way with his team of ten men, and they will move along the south side of the runway, Major Billings will move Alpha troop along the north side of the runway opposite Bravo troop, and both troops will give each other cover.

They reach the eastern end of the runway, and then they came to a holt for a quick recce on the area in front of them, as Chack, had informed them, the Etendard jets were back past the hard standing areas and parked up just inside a small group of houses making the attack a little more difficult, the four Dagger aircraft were missing, the teams had now presumed that they had taken off, but there was now confusion as they would not have left during the night, so they must have gone during the daytime and not returned or transferred to another base.

Alpha and Bravo troop will now combine together and will attempt to destroy the four Etendard aircraft that are parked by the houses.

Billings takes his men over the runway to meet up with Rasheed, and the two officers look over towards the Etendard jets.

The fence had been taken down and a temporary hard road had been built so that the aircraft could be pushed into position next to some houses, the gap in the fence was just about wide enough to take an aircraft through and it had about six men guarding it.

Looking around, the two officers could see that there seemed to be about three or four men guarding each aircraft. The Argentinians knew that the aircraft would well be attacked at some point, so they moved them in between the houses and have a heavy guard around them, but hopefully not enough to delay the SAS team from there attack.

There was no way around this current situation, they would have to launch an assault on the Argentine troops that were around the aircraft, the assault would have to be quick and decisive, and they had to make sure that they could not send out any warning shots that would be heard by the Argentinians.

There was also another danger, were these conscripted troops or were these Marines or special forces that were around the aircraft. Major Billings considered the attack and wanted to do it with all possibility to be as silent as they could be, but these four aircraft were the main target, and they had to be destroyed even if it meant the men were compromised during the attack.

The six Argentinian men at the gate, would be the first target and Captain Rasheed with Bravo troop will move forward to engage them. They radio their intention to Colonel Bradley who has now approached the aircraft hangar with Charlie and Delta troop and they are slowly moving into their advance position.

And then before anyone moved into any position the runway lights came on illuminating the area, every SAS man dropped down and took cover, and at the same time they were keeping one eye closed so that they would not lose their naturel night vision because of the lights.

They all waited for either an aircraft to start up and leave or for an aircraft to return to the base, and now five minutes had gone past and nothing, no sound or sight of any aircraft, everyone was anxious at what they were to expect, and then the lights went back out again, and the entire based was covered in darkness once more.

All the SAS men waited for a further five minutes just to make sure it was safe to move forward again and also to give their eyes a chance to adjust to the darkness once again.

Contact was made between the four assault troops and the mission would continue. Rasheed moved forward with his men towards the fence where the six Argentine soldiers were now all grouped together, two were smoking cigarettes and the other four were now stood relaxed with there FN rifles either slung over the shoulder, or held in the hand low to there side, Bravo troops were now approaching all ten men were spread out in a line and all ten men had there MP5SD sub machine guns in their shoulders in the ready position as they moved forward the men had also put on their black balaclavas to give them a maximum dark covering of their faces.

Bravo trop were now one hundred and fifty metres out from their target, they had been spread out in a line as they made their way across the grass ground towards the hard standings, but now they have now found that the ground here was boggy and hard going so the troop had to move together back onto the transit road from the hard standings to the runway and walk in single file towards the target.

Once over the small bridge that had been built they moved back into a spearhead approach towards the target, and now they had reached the first hard standing and they were within eighty metres of the fence and the Argentine soldiers, Bravo troop wanted to be as close as possible to have a effective fire with the MP5SD weapons, because these weapons are silenced and use the 9 mm rounds there effective range is shorter and the muzzle velocity is also a lot lower so they moved into a closer formation and moved forward towards their targets.

The Argentine soldiers were totally unaware of the approaching SAS men, and they were all together having a chat, to one and another, there were no officers or senior ranks around in control of the men, so they had a little bit of time to relax and break the boredom of the cold night, as they stood together a few of them then shared out their cigarettes, and had a smoke, they all kept their feet moving to keep some warmth in their feet and legs.

None of the Argentine soldiers were equipped with night vision but they did have a few background lights behind them that shined onto the airfield, this also indicated to Bravo troop that these Argentinian soldiers were just conscripts, and did not have the luxury of being offered advanced kit like night vision equipment, every now and again one of the men that was positioned further back around the aircraft would call out something to keep some friendly banter going amongst the men to relieve the night watch they all laughed out and started to shout back some reply.

One of the Argentine soldiers who was getting near to the end of his cigarette had walked forward a little, and was now looking over into the airfield in front of him, for a moment he thought that he could see something moving around out there, maybe it was just a plastic bag he thought, as he tried to look deeper into the darkness and into the airfield, he continued to stare for a few minutes when a Argentine soldier called Cabrera called over to him, 'what is the matter,' he asked.

'Nothing, I thought that I had seen something moving out there,' the soldier answered. He then dropped his cigarette onto the floor and stepped onto it and twisted with his foot, the wind blew up some sparks that danced across the floor, and he then had one more look into the darkness too see if he could see anything again, but he could not see anything, he turned to the rest of the Soldiers and walked the few steps back towards them and joined them for a little bit more banter.

Bravo team were now within thirty metres of the six men, and they were slowly closing, the nearer they got the better the hitting power of the 9 mm rounds, they had just paused and waited for the one soldier to put out his cigarette and turn back towards the others, it was now or never, the ten men of Bravo troop were lined up and ready to fire, they stood firm with their MP5SD sub machine guns firmly into their shoulders ready to fire and looking through there night vision scopes at their targets, as soon as Rasheed gave the order 'Fire' they were all aiming at there targets, each man had his own separate target to hit, and they all fired with a double tap, the muffled sound from the silenced weapons *Phtt, phtt, phtt,* drifted away in the wind that blew across the base along with the soke from the barrels of there weapons, the six Argentine soldiers dropped down to the ground, one seemed to pick up his FN and looked as if he was going to fire it, but he was hit again with a small volley of 9 mm rounds.

Bravo troop now moved quickly forward towards the fence, keeping low as they moved, Alpha troop were now behind them and moving in. They now had to move into the streets to gain access to the aircraft, that were also being guarded by Argentine soldiers, these soldiers seemed to be a little more awake as they had there FN rifles up ready, and in their shoulders, as they moved around keeping watch over their prized aircraft.

The SAS men now faced a problem, they would now have to carefully take out the sentries around the aircraft and plant their explosives, but the Argentine soldiers were moving around, and they looked ready for any assault, and as the aircraft were scattered and not together, this would be a little bit more difficult.

Captain Rasheed and Major Billings had decided that Bravo troop would move forward and take care of the sentries and Alpha troop would then plant the explosives inside the aircraft, this also presented another issue, if they take down the Argentine sentries then they would have to put a shorter fuse in the explosives, because if anyone was to walk around the corner and see the sentries down they would automatically realise that the aircraft were set to explode, so as soon as they were destroyed the better.

They will therefore also fit an anti tamper device so if anyone attempts to pull the detonator out, the device will then go off and the C4 would explode early.

CHAPTER EIGHT.

While Bravo and Alpha troop were busy on the Eastern end of the runway, Charlie and Delta troop had now formed up just outside the western end of the runway, there targets were the anti-aircraft gun emplacements to the southern side of the airbase and also the aircraft hangar that held the four Exocet missiles, and also the four Skyhawk jets that were parked outside by the hangar, they would also look at the underground bunker and see what kind of damage could be done to that as well.

Colonel Bradley had radioed Sergeant Major Owen who was in charge of the ten men in HQ troop who were at the Land Rovers, and he had asked the Sergeant Major to move two of the Land Rovers forward so that they faced the western end of the base just in case they would need any covering fire from the GPMG machine guns that were mounted to the Land Rovers.

With the six men that the Squadron Sergeant Major had with him he moved three Land rovers into place giving a little bit extra cover just in case leaving four men on guard watching the roads to there west.

So far, the raid had gone well, and they had not disturbed anyone, up until now, in fact the news from the two Hercules, and the two sentry points indicated that there were no problems and no traffic had been seen on the road.

The Argentine soldiers that were living in the small barracks at the airbase were all asleep, they had three soldiers that were selected for the night time guard duty, and these men were armed, and patrolling around the outside of the barracks, joining up every now and then having a stop for a chat and a cigarette, tonight was the same as any other night, and that any raid by British forces was now looking very unlikely, and as a result there was more of a relaxed atmosphere again within the camp, and again a bit of time for a cigarette a chat and some well aimed banter .

Meanwhile the underground bunkers at the airbase were being manned by Argentine officers who were not only working in there, but also sleeping in there as well, they were monitoring all things around the base, and at one point someone had reported seeing something low down on the radar, but after a while nothing showed up again, so they decided that it must have been a large flock of birds that had taken flight over to the west and then landed again at a new location, this was a common occurrence within the area, even though they had a similar event on the eastern side of the base out over the Ocean just a few nights before with the mystery rumble that the people in the city were talking about.

There were five anti-aircraft emplacements on this side of the airbase and only three would create any kind of problem for the mission, there were also another three to the north of the base that so far had been ignored as they did not present a large threat to the current mission like the others had down so.

Colonel Bradley had therefore decided not to take these guns out, but just concentrate on the ones that were a direct threat to the mission, the three anti aircraft guns that were in the area of the hangar and the aircraft parked on the apron.

The first gun emplacement was near to the old foundations that Chack had used for cover on several occasions, on his recce missions and when he visited the field kitchen, again the gun was surrounded by a berm that had been built up, and there were three men inside with a 20 mm twin barrel RH 202 Mk 20 anti-aircraft machine gun, capable of firing one thousand rounds per minute and can be quickly used to put down fire on ground troops if needed, and has a range of two thousand metres and this could also reach the two Hercules if they turn close enough to the airbase when they take-off.

Delta troop will move forward, towards the first gun emplacement and the ten men team led by Captain Len Smith, would move into the remains of the foundations of the old buildings, Captain Smith had kept his men low, and when they reached the foundations they would then crawl along the old foundations, however Delta troop come across another problem, and that was that they have now discovered another gun emplacement just to the north of the target, one that Chack had missed or one that had recently been added. It was not certain, but the Argentinians may even be setting up extra gun emplacements in the area or even just moving the existing ones around.

A decision has to be made quick, and Colonel Bradley has now sent Charlie troop in towards the second gun emplacement, they would have to be taken out, both together at the same time, Delta troop have decided to go in and use there knives in there attack, and to do it in complete silence, they move five men towards the berm and these men will slide up the side and over the top of the berm and attack the three men in the gun emplacement, they will be given cover from the other five SAS men of Delta troop who will be ready with there MP5SD sub machine guns.

The five men have there knives out ready as they slowly move up the berm, they then check the position of the three gun crew below them, one is currently sat in the chair of the anti-aircraft gun and the other two are sat on each side, one is asleep the other is smoking and the man in the chair is looking around at the night sky.

The five Delta troop men then slipped over the top of the berm, and launched there attack on the three men, the one on the gun was the priority target, just in case he fired a volley of rounds off and woke the air base and the city up, he was quickly delt with, with a Kabar knife blade across the throat, the one who was asleep was finished before he even woke up but the third man managed to knock his attacker down with a blow from his rifle butt, and he had managed to turn his weapon on his attacker before he was hit with a number of rounds in the head from the Delta troop who were giving cover fire showering two of the Delta knife team in blood an matter as the 9mm rounds hit their target.

This gun emplacement was now completely neutralised, and as it was hit, Charlie troop moved onto the other gun emplacement, and this time with there silenced MP5SD sub machine guns they shot the two men who were manning a 7.62 mm GPMG that was fitted to a SF tripod (Sustained fire) the two men were quickly taken out with a group of double tap hits to the head sending a cloud of red mist into the night sky.

Colonel Bradley had again looked at his watch the mission was going along smoothly but he was anxious to get it done and get everyone out of here as soon as possible before anyone on the base started to notice any Argentine men down.

As Delta and Charlie troops move forward, they are now finding that there are some more gun emplacements around, Colonel Bradley stopped the two troops and has now decided to put three men onto the 20 mm gun that they had just taken out with the knives, and they can then use it for covering fire for the rest of the men, just in case they get discovered, so now Delta and Charlie will combine as they move forward.

There are two more gun emplacements that will need to be neutralised before the troop can move on to the hangar. They now move towards the next gun and again this is a 20 mm twin barrel RH 202 gun with a three man crew, the SAS troop decide to just run through the position fast and using there silenced weapons, and to take out the gun as fast as possible, they get ready, and then get up and move quick the first five men are grouped together as they come to the berm where the gun is placed, they move fast, and silent, and then dive onto the berm and at the same time all five men fire onto the three men with double tap precision, the three men are hit before they knew that they had been attacked. The men now move quickly forward using stealth, and speed ready to take the next gun position, again this was another 20 mm twin barrelled RH 202 anti-aircraft gun, and again the three men were hit with a volley of accurate double tap head shots, and with blood everywhere the Argentine men drop to the ground, the SAS men could now turn and head towards the hangar and the four Skyhawk jets that were parked on the apron next to the hangar

As the SAS troop were running towards the fence one of the SAS men had sworn that he had seen a trench to the one side as he ran past, but there had not been any response from anyone inside the trench, they had now reached the fence perimeter that was around the hangar and the apron, and they had now taken cover, the SAS trooper that had seen the trench, had now mentioned the fact of the possible trench to Colonel Bradley, who had taken note of the fact, as he was convinced that so far they had been lucky in the defences that they had come across, and also the fact that they had not come across larger anti-aircraft weapons that he thought would have been here on the base. Colonel Bradley had decided that their withdrawal should be by a better route, out of the base maybe back up and along the runway towards the west and out that way.

They were now next to the aircraft hangar here the Exocets were stored, and the area was in darkness at the moment, but there were sentries walking around the area. The information from Chack was that some of the sentries were actually regular troops like Marines, who were equipped with night vision. As Colonel Bradley looked on past the hangar he could see the outline of a number of aircraft, these must be the Skyhawks, but there seemed to be two other aircraft parked here and these looked like two of the Dagger fighter bombers, he concluded that there must have been a mission earlier in the day, and that four Daggers went out and only two returned.

Now they had to get into the hangar and

over to the aircraft they had sentries to deal with as well, things will start to get tricky once they enter the apron area.

There are two guards at the gate, the troop can either go through the gate or cut there way through the fence Colonel Bradley looked at his watch, he was anxious that they did not spend too long on the mission, he had also just been relayed a message that the underground bunkers should be left and not attacked, the worry now was that political damage from the death of a bunch of high ranking officers could lose the Country, and the Prime Minister vital support for the war on the Falklands. In a way the decision was a relief, it was one less part of the mission to worry about. Colonel Bradley was now worrying about the two troops on the other side of the air base as he had not heard from them for a while.

*

Meanwhile over on the other side of the air base Alpha and Bravo troop were now slowly moving in around the first aircraft, Bravo troop were busy watching the three sentries around the first Etendard aircraft, they decide to take the three sentries out silently with knives, Sergeant Billy Ballantine, moved forward as a volunteer to deal with the sentries. Billy was known better in the Regiment as the surgeon, as he had the knack of pushing his knife into the precise spot where the carotid artery ran through the left of the neck, he preferred the Fairbairn Sykes blade as it was nice long and sharp, and it would slide into a neck nice and easy.

Billy was also good at sneaking around and as he watched the three sentries, two would seem to stay at the front of there aircraft while the other one would walk down and around the rear of the aircraft. The aircraft were covered with green skim camouflage nets so that they would not be easily seen from the air, but the nets provided shadows that Billy would take advantage of.

Billy sneaked in towards the aircraft and then went down under the wing of the aircraft, he then waited for the Argentine soldier to walk past the wing towards the rear of the jet, all the time the Argentine soldier was looking out and away from the aircraft, watching all around, Billy then got to his feet and then without any real speed, he slowly crept up on the soldier, and then grabbed him from behind with his right arm, and then putting his left hand over the man's mouth.

Billy then pulled the man back, and gently pushed his Fairbairn Sykes blade deep into the Argentine soldiers neck. and held him still while the carotid bleed out, death came quick, and Billy slowly and quietly pulled the body back and placed it under the aircraft in the shadows and out of the way.

Billy then moved slowly forward and waited for the one guard to move away, as soon as the soldier moved around the side of the aircraft, Billy would strike once again and again follow the same pattern, he would grab the man from behind with his right hand and place his hand over the man's mouth and pull his head back and then insert his knife deep into the man's neck and hold him until all life had gone and let the blood flow from the man's neck.

At the same time, one of the other SAS men had delt with the final guard, this time a fast movement, and just like Billy had done he would grab the man from behind and put his hand over his mouth, but this time he pulled the man's head back and with his razor sharp Kabar knife he slashed the knife deep across the soldiers throat, a shower of red blood erupted from the man and as the blood ran out a cloud of steam also made its way up out of the Argentine soldiers body as the warm blood found the cold winter air.

This was the first aircraft clear, they now had to move onto the other three aircraft all with three men looking after each aircraft. Again, they would have to put there killing skills to the test.

They moved past the house and onto the next aircraft, and as they did, Alpha troop followed would then follow them, and the men of Alpha troop set up cover positions ready to engage any Argentine soldiers that may happen to walk into the area. And they also prepared the explosives to place inside the aircraft. Two kilos of C4 will be used on each aircraft, complete with a two litre bottle of diesel oil for the incendiary effect, and the explosives are made up by two men who have chosen an old school method of timed detonator with a number ten delay pencil detonator, but they also use an old trick to make the detonator ant tamper, so if someone does try and de activate it, it will blow up while they try.

The two men will place the explosives inside the air intake of each aircraft about two feet inside so that it will do maximum structural damage to the aircraft, and its electronics, along with the fuel capacity and engine intake. They have set the pencil detonators to go off in thirty minutes in all hope that they will be over the other side of the airbase and running towards the Hercules before they go off.

The explosives men would crimp the end of the detonator, and that would crush a glass vial inside the detonator that was filled with Cupric chloride, this would then start to corrode a wire inside that was holding back a spring striker, once the wire had corroded the striker would strike forward into the detonator and this would then set off the explosion with the C4.

Meanwhile Bravo troop were now moving quick through the sentries around the aircraft, they had now cleared three of the aircraft, and when they reached the final aircraft, they were surprised to find that the three men that should have been guarding it had vanished.

Bravo troop moved around in an all around defensive position while the men of Alpha troop moved in, and the two explosive men planted the last of there C4 and replaced the inlet cover on the last aircraft.

The men were now finished at this site and could now move back towards the fence and back onto the airfield.

*

At the same time Colonel Bradley and his men were now moving around towards the aircraft hangar, they have now launched an attack on the two men at the gate firing there silenced MP5SD weapons on the two Argentine guards, they then moved in towards the hangar where the two explosives men were making ready to plant their C4 onto the Exocet missiles, there was a side door at the hangar that they use to could gain entry through, and three men went forward to enter the building and clear it of any Argentine soldiers, they could see four men inside all of them were armed, there were some lights on as well so the SAS men had to sneak in slowly. The SAS men kept there MP5SD weapons in their shoulders and aiming out, they were all ready to fire once they had their targets in sight, the Argentine soldiers had not heard the SAS men enter the building, and so far, they were totally unaware of the three men moving around the inside of the hangar. The Argentine men were stood chatting and not really ready for any attack, so when it came, they did not expect it. The three SAS men now had a clear view and a clear field of fire onto the Argentine soldiers inside of the hangar, and now they opened fire on them before they could react cutting all four men down.

So far everything was going to plan but with the rounds being fired inside the hangar, two rounds had hit the outer wall with a bit of a clatter.

This had now alerted some of the soldiers that were on guard around the Skyhawk Jets and also Dagger aircraft, and they have now started to move forward cautiously to see what had happened.

The SAS men had taken cover in the dark shadows, but two Argentine soldiers had night vision scopes fitted to there rifles and one of them had spotted someone hiding inside one of the shadows and now he fired off a round at him.

Fortunately, the round had just missed but the sound of a round would now alert everyone on the base, and now the SAS men had no choice but to put down a wall of intense fire with there MP5SD sub machine guns cutting down the Argentine soldiers, as the SAS men moved forward to run through the Argentine guards.

Meanwhile the explosives were now set on the Exocets along with the anti tamper devices, and the two explosives men were now heading outside and were heading towards the aircraft, that were parked upon the apron.

They worked as fast as they could and placed their explosives inside the air intakes of each aircraft but did not have enough explosives with them for the two Dagger aircraft that were parked up next to them, as the explosives for these aircraft would have been with Bravo troop who were on the other side of the airbase.

Colonel Bradley was now calling all men in towards the hangar except the men he left on the 20 mm anti-aircraft gun who would give the rest of them cover.

So far nothing seemed to have stirred at the base, maybe by some miracle no one had heard the shot, and now all the explosives were now fixed to the aircraft and missiles and set, and now all the troops could now get back together and head back to the Hercules for their exit. All the men were now in a defensive position covering each other just in case of an Argentine attack.

Alpha and Bravo troop were now through the fence, and they were making their way back towards the runway and back towards the hangar where they will join with the rest of SAS men.

Then just as they were about ten metres away from the runway, the runway lights had been switched on, the men dropped to the ground to take cover, and all lay there in a prone position.

In the background behind them Alpha and Bravo troop could now hear shouting from Argentine men running through the streets behind them, this shouting would now increase in volume as they stumble upon the dead Argentine soldiers that were lay under the aircraft.

'Okay all, we may as well switch to the noisy weapons, we have been discovered,' Rasheed said as he prepared his men for a fight, they all made there MP5SD weapons safe and then made the CAR 15 rifles ready for use. They could also now see vehicle head lights around the outside of the base, this must be Argentine reinforcements coming in. The two troops had heard the single gunshot and knew if they had heard it everyone else in the area would have heard it as well.

CHAPTER NINE.

Northwood.

A message had been sent to Northwood informing them that the explosives had been set and would blow in thirty minutes, The Director, was delighted with the news, at least just doing this would be a major victory against the Argentine Junta, the PM will be delighted he thought to himself when he heard the news.

Colonel Cedric was still looking at the messages for the latest updates when Mikado could broadcast them. He was happy that Colonel Bradley and his men had been on the ground for just under one hour and have so far gone through there mission with a steady speed, he was now hoping to hear the news that they were on their way back to the two Hercules and on there way out of Argentina.

The Director was now patting Colonel Thomas on the back, 'you made this possible Bill, with that young man you placed in there,' Colonel Thomas was feeling proud at this moment, but he was also a little bit cautious about any kind of celebration, he knew that after all this his head will still be on the block anyway, for going behind everyone's back in the Regiment, and putting a man on the ground at Rio Grande.

*

Back in Rio Grande things were now starting too hot up a little, Alpha and Bravo troop had moved away towards the north of the runway and were now running along the side of the runway towards the western end, just as the Argentinians were now waking up and starting to respond to the gunfire.

'Maybe they will just think it was a mistaken discharge' Major Austin commented to Colonel Bradley.

'They will not think that for very long John, not once the Argentine radio messages are not responded too, we need to get out of here, and get out fast.'

Colonel Bradley was looking for a way out and the only way he could see was out towards the runway and back down that way, but he also had three men to get out who were left manning the 20 mm RH 202 anti-aircraft gun on the north side next to the barracks and hangar.

'John get the men to change over to the CAR 15 rifles, I think we can say our cover will be blown, so we ay as well go out with a bang,' Colonel Bradley said as he looked towards a way out in the west of the base.

Now they could hear heavy footfall in the darkness, as men started to come out of the barracks and run around in the shadows. The Argentines fired two rounds towards the SAS men at the hangar, and now this prompted the three SAS men on the 20 RH 202 to come into action, and they did with a number of bursts on the machine gun towards the Argentine troops heading out of the barracks and towards the hangar, this gun fire had now started to confuse some of the Argentine soldiers as they could not work out why their own guns would be firing onto them.

Trooper Micky Watkins was on the trigger with the RH 202, it was one of the weapons that he had learnt about on the build up to the mission, where every man learns what weapons the enemy have in their arsenal, and then they are trained to use those weapons if they are behind enemy lines and come across them.

Micky was an excellent shot with the weapon, and he had now placed down a number of accurate burst that had either chopped down the Argentine soldiers or made then go for cover, he then turned the gun towards the barracks and placed a number of heavy bursts into the building hoping to inflict some major damage and keep any troops from coming out of there and joining the battle.

With the fire going down onto the Argentine troops it gave Colonel Bradley time to move the two troops that were with him up towards the runway to try and make and escape.

The three men on the 20 mm anti-aircraft

gun could now see a group of trucks heading up the road towards the airbase from the town, they now turned the gun towards the trucks, and now with accurate aiming and fire they started to put down a barrage of fire towards the trucks, they hit the first truck, but the other two trucks pulled up and the men inside the trucks all jumped out and were now putting down small arms fire towards Micky Watkins and his gun crew.

Micky Watkins and his crew on the 20 mm gun now knew that the Argentines had sussed out that the gun was now in enemy hands and that they would have to do a quick exit soon.

Colonel Bradley and his men were now coming under fire from the Argentine men that had made their way around the other side of the barracks away from the 20 mm gun fire that was raining onto them and were now firing at Colonel Bradley and his men. They now started to return fire on the Argentine men, but Colonel Bradley had the problem of having the runway lights on behind him and giving away his position by making them look like silhouettes.

In the meantime, Captain Rasheed and Major Billings had taken Alpha and Bravo troop to the western end of the runway. The two troops were now taking over the two RH 202 twin barrelled 20 mm anti-aircraft guns at the end of the runway, the SAS men had jumped in and pulled the dead Argentine bodies out and laid them out next to the gun emplacements. Major Billings was now using his binoculars to pick out the main concentrations of muzzle flash from the advancing Argentine troops, coming around from the back of the barracks.

Major Billings had now found a large concentration of Argentine troops firing from a gap between the barrack building, and the hangar and then ran around behind the gun where three of his men were now in position to start using the weapon, they had lowered the barrel down and now with Major Billings instructions they have made, for a rough aim to where he had guided them.

The trigger was slowly pushed down by the SAS man's left foot, and a short burst fired into the direction, that Major billings had given to the men, Major Billings was watching the strike from the tracers and then called out an adjustment to his men who altered the hight of the gun and then fired off another burst.

'Bang on boys, hit them with all we have got' Major Billings yelled, and at that the SAS gun team put down a fierce wall of fire into the selected target. Major Billings watched as the rounds hit the target area and watched as the tracers were bouncing around spinning up and off over into the air field, and then hitting the ground, and then going up high into the night sky looking like red comets as they soared towards the clouds.

The large amount of fire that was coming from that area had now ceased the gun had done its job.

The SAS men were now seeking mass amounts of Argentine muzzle flashes, and then they were putting down as much fire onto those areas as possible, there aim was to pile up the casualties, the more enemy they hit the more the morale of the Argentine troops would falter.

At the same time that Major Billings had taken over the one gun, Captain Rashed had taken over the other gun with his men that was just on the other side of the runway, They were now coming under fire from a number of anti-aircraft guns positioned in the northern part of the air base, these were positions that they knew about but did not need to assault as they were out of the way of the Mikado mission, there was one enemy gun position at six hundred metres and another at eleven hundred metres, both guns were 20 mm and the nearest one was a single barrel while the furthest was a double barrelled gun, Rasheed and his men aimed up first, at the closest gun, and after about five long bursts from there RH 202 they silenced the first gun with a number of heavy accurate bursts of fire, they then quickly turned the gun and offered there full attention to the gun furthest away, and now they started to put down some heavy, immense fire onto the Argentine gun position, it took some time but with accurate calculating Rasheed managed to guide his men in, and hit the gun with direct hits, even though the Argentine gun crew were getting closer to hitting the SAS men at the same time, the SAS men managed to set their aim and fire much more quickly than the Argentinians had.

The rest of Alpha and Bravo troop were now moving into a position at the south western end of the airfield so that they could give covering fire for the withdrawing SAS troops, in the mean time Sergeant Major Owen had moved the three Land Rovers up to the south western edge of the airfield. and had them now positioned so that the GPMG machine guns mounted on the Land Rovers could put down fire on the Argentine troops.

*

Major Castillo was awakened from his sleep 'Sir we are being attacked by the British,'

Major Castillo who was in command of a reserve group, that were elements of the 602 Commando Company that were currently fighting on the Falkland Islands, he and his reserve group were currently awaiting transfer to the Islands.

Major Castillo jumped up out of his bed and got started to quickly get dressed, he was talking as he did so. 'Tell me what has happened,' he asked the young Corporal.

'The British have attacked the base sir; we do not know where they had attacked from, they just appeared at the base.'

'Okay so they may well have parachuted into the base, so these will be paratroopers or special forces,' Major Castillo replied as he thought about the situation and was pulling on his boots.

'Are all my men awake.'

'Yes, Major they are awake and getting ready as we speak.'

The Major left his room in a hurried walk all the time shouting out to his men to get ready and armed.

The Major had twenty men at hand, some of the best Marines, they were only twenty minutes away from the Rio Grande airbase, and they were north of the base so will have to drive along the coastal road to get to the airbase so would need to go through some of the suburbs of Rio Grande.

Major Castillo ordered his men to be armed and ready, to leave in three minutes, the two trucks had arrived to pick them up, and as he requested his men were already armed, and to leave.

The Marines climbed up into the trucks and were now leaving their temporary camp and heading along the road to the Rio Grande airbase, each Marine was preparing his equipment, loading rifle magazines, and doing their final checks to their weapons, ready to engage the enemy as the trucks rolled along the road.

It was now 01.18 and the Marines had now reached the airbase, they were travelling along the eastern road along the sea front, and then they would turn and come up along road on the south side of the air base. Just as they turned into the southern road there was a large explosion followed by another one on the south western edge of the base, the truck stopped and the Marines jumped out to witness a large fireball heading up into the night sky, at this time they did not realise what had happened but another truck on the road in front of them had just been hit by 20 mm rounds from a RH202 anti-aircraft gun.

*

Colonel Bradley had just witnessed the explosion on the south western corner of the airbase, the first Etendard had exploded, and now the aviation fuel has ignited sending flames high into the air, about one minute after that, the second Etendard had now exploded and again with the aviation fuel going up with it there was another large fireball mushroom cloud headed up into the dark night sky.

For a moment the shooting seemed to have died down as everyone looked over towards the explosions, but then the firing intensified again.

Sergeant Major Owen and his men on the Land Rovers were now putting down sustained fire from there GPMG, s and were now giving Micky Watkins and his crew, enough fire cover to now abandon their Argentine Anti-Aircraft gun and now start to withdraw towards the rest of the SAS team at the western end of the airbase.

However, the firing from the three Land Rovers had now attracted the fire from a .50 calibre, single barrel anti-aircraft gun, the gun was well aimed and hit one of the Land Rovers and hit the two men that were on there firing the GPMG. The two SAS men were hit with a number of rounds, and both died instantly.

The single gun now attracted the attention of Major Billings and his gun team on the runway who now turned and began to put down heavy fire onto the position, but it seemed that the position was well, dug in, and they just could not get the rounds into it to silence it.

Trooper Harris and Smithy however grabbed a Milan missile launcher from the rear of one of the Land Rovers and ran over to the northern road, they now had a clear view from there, of the Argentine gun emplacement, and the two Argentine soldiers who were manning the gun. Harris and Smithy had quickly prepared the Milan launcher and placed a rocket onto it and with the careful eye of Harris using the night vision sight on the Milan, they locked onto their target and fired, the missile launched and then with a whoosh it shoot off at high speed, and shot across the airbase straight into the single gun emplacement, there followed a white flash and a large boom as the missile exploded sending soil Argentine men and the gun itself into the night sky.

At the same time another Etendard had exploded at the south eastern end of the runway, and as had exploded and the bright ball of fire headed up into the sky, it was then followed by the fourth and last Etendard exploding, and two large fireballs were heading into the sky almost together.

Captain Rasheed was now putting down fire on the Argentine troops that were making there way along the northern edge of the runway, with the battle raging the Argentinians had now realised that the runway lights were in fact acting against themselves by lighting up their own men and making them easy targets for the SAS soldiers to shot at, the decision was made to switch the lights off.

With the darkness came a lull in the fighting while everyone started to get used to the darkness or if they had any night vision equipment, they quickly switched on their night vision, however just as the lights went off there was a huge flash and a series of explosions from the hangar as the explosives that were placed onto the Exocet missiles went off, this was an even bigger explosion and blew the side of the hangar wall down with it.

With the light from the explosion of the hangar, and the accompanying fire illuminating the area Captain Rasheed could now see the two Dagger jets that were parked on the apron, the SAS men that assaulted these aircraft did not have enough explosive to place charges on the two Dagger aircraft, so Colonel Bradley had advised Rasheed that if he could see the aircraft then try and damage them.

Rasheed ordered his gun group to turn their gun and with a few shots to zero in on the two Dagger aircraft they then aimed, and then they turned their gun and opened fire on the two Dagger jets putting dozens of rounds into each one, as they did so the four Skyhawks suddenly exploded as their planted C4 charges went off.

All aircraft and missiles were now all destroyed the mission was now a success, but the battle here at the airbase was now far from being over, now Major Castillo had turned up and his Marines were moving into the fight and Castillo was dragging in conscripts to engage in the fight under his command.

With the ammunition on the two anti-aircraft guns now virtually gone Rasheed and Billings had now called their men to start to move over towards the north western end and towards the Land Rovers, time was ticking, and they needed to move towards the aircraft and make there exit, there job here was now done.

The withdrawal of the SAS men was not going to be so easy, with Major Castillo and his few Marines now at the battle, Castillo was commandeering ordinary Argentine soldiers and now organising them into groups, Castillo was trying to work out how the British had got here, he knew they will try and run for the border with Chile or maybe they have helicopters somewhere or boats but the run to Chile would be the most obvious.

Castillo decided he needed to try and prevent them from escaping the area, he sent two Marines with a group of twenty Argentine conscripts up the southern road to try and cut off any escape, Castillo thought that the fire power from a concentrated mass of twenty men would be enough to prevent any escape.

The Argentine soldiers sneaked up along the edge of the southern road, keeping well low inside the shadows, the group of Argentine soldiers reached two hundred metres towards the junction where the burning Land Rover was positioned, and with the other two Land Rovers that were giving covering fire onto the battle field.

Major Billings and Captain Rasheed were now moving across to the main group of SAS men. The Argentine group was now at one hundred metres away, it was now that the Marine Sergeant had got the men in line ready to open fire.

'Fuego' the sergeant shouted, and his men fired upon the SAS men, most of the first rounds missed there intended target however one SAS man caught a round in his upper leg, Rasheed had seen the muzzle flashes and quickly took command of the fire and ordered a barrage of fire into the area where he had seen the muzzle flashes. Half of the Argentine men were hit in the intense barrage of gunfire from the SAS men and their CAR 15 rifles, at the same time Sergeant Major Owen had turned the GPMG he was using around, and now he had put down about one hundred rounds into the area where he could see the muzzle flashes. The result was carnage, and the rest of the Argentine group were all hit with multiple rounds from the onslaught of fire.

The SAS men had now regrouped into small sections, and each were concentrating their fire power down onto the remaining Argentinians that were still in the fight. The time now was 01.44 and Colonel Bradley wanted to make a withdrawal back to the Hercules he knew every minute on the ground will put a risk onto the two Hercules aircraft.

The men moved back across towards the South western corner and towards there exit road that headed back west towards the two Hercules aircraft. Colonel Bradley had managed to radio the two Hercules, and he had asked them to transmit to Northwood that all the aircraft at the airbase had now been destroyed, and the four Exocet missiles that were located inside the hangar, have all been destroyed as well. At this point he did not mention the SAS casualties, so far two dead and one wounded.

The two bodies of the dead SAS men were picked up and loaded onto one of the Land Rovers along with the wounded trooper, and then made ready to move out back towards the aircraft.

The SAS men now made themselves into groups so that they could lay down a fire and manoeuvre withdrawal, back to the road, and then back towards the two Hercules aircraft, they all knew that even more Argentine troops would be arriving at the air base at any moment, and if they did not move now, they would soon be bogged down inside an un winnable battle.

CHAPTER TEN.

Northwood.

The Director of special forces was sat with Colonel Thomas and Colonel Cedric, they were all awaiting any news from Rio Grande, and the SAS mission at the airbase to destroy the aircraft and the remaining Exocet missiles.

So far, the mission had gone well, but there was an eerie radio silence at the moment, and no one knew what was currently happening at the Argentine airbase, the three men were all sat there drinking coffee, none of them were talking, they were just listening for any sign that a signal had come in with an update.

'Sir,' One of the signalman called out, and at that all three of the officers jumped out of there seats and headed over to the young man with the earphones on his head.

'What is it,' the DSF asked him.

The young man paused for a moment and then with a slight smile he looked up at the officers and said, 'Confirmation all aircraft and Exocet missiles have been destroyed at the airbase at Rio

Grande.'

There was a cheer from the three officers who were delighted by the news, they were now patting each other on the back and looking totally relieved that the mission had been a success.

At this point there also was no another transmission on the current casualties, and also on the current gun battle at the base, as the SAS men had come under intense fire from the Argentine defenders, there surprise element had now been compromised by a single gunshot, what Colonel Bradley was hoping for was a silent mission, just a in and out raid without disturbing anyone, but instead there was a full scale battle down at the Rio Grande airbase, so much so that the minster has just turned up, and he has demanded to speak with the Director.

The Director looked a little puzzled by the fact that the Minister was there demanding to see him, but at least he could give him the good news about the Exocets missiles.

'Good morning, Minister, I am surprised to see you this early in the morning,' The Director said as he entered the room where the Minster was awaiting his arrival.

'What is gong on at Rio Grande,' the Minister asked going straight to the point.

'We have just destroyed the Etendard and Exocet missiles,' the Director replied with a large grin.

'Well, I have just been woken up and informed by the Argentine ambassador, that there is in fact a large force of British soldiers on the base, and that there are heavy casualties, and heavy fighting,'

The Director was taken back by the comments, this was the first he had heard about any battle at the base, 'I am sorry Minister, but we have not been informed about any battle.'

'The whole war down there is being held together by delicate diplomatic threads, if other countries hear about some kind of invasion, then there will be all kinds of diplomatic problems,' the minster said as he was pacing up and down the room.

'I will send a signal and try and get some confirmation on this news,' At that the Director left the office and made his way to the ops room to get the signaller to send a message asking about any fight.

The two Colonels walked over, 'Anything wrong,' Colonel Cedric asked.

'The Minister has been awoken by the Argentine ambassador, apparently there is some kind of gun battle down at Rio Grande.'

The three officers await a return signal, and after five minutes one comes through. *'There has been an attack by Argentine forces, we have inflicted many casualties onto the Argentine force, and we have taken some casualties ourselves, two dead and one wounded,'* was the return encrypted message.

'Fuck it,' the Director shouted when he had

heard the news. He then headed back to the room where the Minister was waiting for him.

The Director pushed the door open with a wide swing and the door hit the wall with a bang, this made the Minister jump up out of his seat, he was taken back by the way the Director had entered the room like he did. 'I have two dead men and one wounded so far, it seems that the Argentinians have mounted a large attack on my men,'

'Two dead,' the Minister said with a tremble in his voice.

'Yes, two dead and one wounded, this is a bloody war man, we did not start it, but we will bloody well end it,' The Director shouted and then paused for a moment as he stared at the minister 'now my good chap, the good news is that the aircraft and missiles are gone, they are no longer a threat to our men, or our ships, and you think about that when that Ambassador comes around moaning to you about a fire fight at his bloody airbase.'

At that the Minister moved towards the door and made an exit, the fear in his eyes from the seeing the Directors temper made him realise not too question anything again.

*

Colonel Bradley had now started a tactical withdrawal, at the moment they have the Argentine soldiers keeping there heads down, but Colonel Bradley knows that with his ammunition running low he can only hang on for so long. The

SAS men make their way back to the Land Rovers and motorcycles parked just down the road and prepare to climb on and make there exit. However, the Argentine Marines have now moved forward in pursuit of the SAS men, they are also being joined by a group of Buzo Tactico special forces assault group who are now running with the Marines in pursuit of the SAS.

When the SAS almost reach their parked motorcycles and Land Rovers they come under fire again from the Argentine forces, and although they thought that they would escape the fight, the fight was actually following close behind them and the Argentinians were not going to be giving up that easy.

Again, the SAS men spread out to meet the attacking Argentine force, but unlike the battle on the airbase the SAS men knew that these were different fighters, there tactics were a lot different, and they were not bunched up like the others were, plus their aim was a lot more accurate and more controlled, instead of multiple rounds being fired they were firing single rounds that were hitting their targets.

The SAS men once again put themselves into small sections, again their aim was to create multiple casualties with immense fire, they were also lucky as the parked Land Rovers that were near to them had a full supply of 7.62 ammunition and guns at the ready to also give them covering fire, they also had there 203 grenade launchers and up to now had not used them, now will be different and they had a good supply of 203 grenades to use.

The Argentines were now putting down a barrage of fire and Captain Rasheed had now noticed a group of Argentinians had sneaked across the to the south and across the land and were now trying to out flank the SAS men, Captain Hastings took eight men and moved to the south in a counter attack. The ground to the north and the south was very boggy and any movement was very limited Hastings knew he could hold off the Argentinian attack, and quickly advance, but he did not realise that he was up against the Buzo Tactico fighters and was surprised at the fire power these men were putting down on his troops, they however turned the game around by firing multiple 203 high explosive grenades at the Argentine men, they fired the grenades to give a max explosive zone landing area so the grenades went off all around the attacking men forcing them back either into a deeper boggy ground or back to the main road that they had just walked from.

The SAS men now had to push there attackers back hard in a relentless counter attack, the harder they fought back the more they would push these Argentine soldiers back, again there aim was to inflict major casualties they knew if they hit a large amount of the Argentinians then the Argentinians would withdraw, and again the SAS used a tactic of accurate shooting at there targets and accurate hitting of the target a one shot one kill tactic that would save on ammunition and inflict major damage, and now it was working and with that tactic and the now immense fire that was being put down by the GPMG's on the Land Rovers it was working well.

Colonel Bradley knew he would not be able to hold off the Argentinians for long enough, and for the two aircraft to leave, there was only one way out and that would be for a holding force to hold back the Argentinian advance, while the rest of the men get on the two Hercules and get out, the remaining team will then have to take their chances and head for the border with Chile.

As soon as the Argentinian force was pushed back then the men will have to take the bikes and Land Rovers and leave two Land Rovers behind for the holding team to make their escape once the two Hercules were airborne.

Ten men have volunteered to remain and fight while the two Hercules go, Colonel Bradley had radioed the aircraft to get ready for a fast take off and he then sent his remaining men back towards the Hercules transports while the ten men held on and kept the Argentinians back.

All the men loaded up into the Land Rovers and jumped up on the motorcycles and reluctantly raced back to the two Hercules, they left the ten men all their ammunition as they did so, and any other kit that they thought they could use, Colonel Bradley, Major Austin and Captain Rasheed remained along with Chack who said he was down here for a week anyway so had a few days to go making most of the men laugh.

The men came under sporadic fire now and then from the Argentinian soldiers who were now moving forward again with more caution and testing the SAS men by taking shots and retreating.

All the other men returned to Omen One and Two who were now all ready with there engines running ready to take off. The SAS men dumped their Land Rovers through the fences at the side of the road next to the two Hercules, and the motorcycle's as well they then carried there two dead brothers onboard and carried the wounded trooper onto the Hercules.

As soon as the men were on board, the pilot of the first Hercules pushed the throttles wide open, the lift off will have to be the shortest they have ever attempted as they will only be low on the ground and will have to turn towards starboard and head south, he will be quickly flowed by Omen Two who will also carry out the same manoeuvre and again he will keep have to keep low to the ground.

Omen, One releases his brakes, and now speeds down the road with only his night vision goggle to see his way, he is pulling on the stick ready to lift and as soon as the Hercules goes light, he knows he is up, he then has to gain just enough hight to make the turn, and so far, he is successful, the pilots keep checking to make sure that they have no missiles coming in at them. Just thirty seconds after Omen One had taken off, then Omen Two lifts off, and she is now turning south behind the first Hercules, both aircraft are up and staying as lo as they had dared to be, not only are the pilots looking in front but they are cautiously looking to the side to make sure that there wing does not hit the ground as they turn at such a low level and try and turn as tight as possible.

Colonel Bradley gave out a sigh of relief as he could hear the two Hercules taking off behind him and looked west to try and get a glimpse of the two aircraft as they passed low to the ground, but he could not see them only hear them, but the relief was not for long, as the Argentinians have now made another attack on the SAS men.

Now a plan has to be made for the ten men to make there escape, they are about thirty miles from the border with Chile and they will have half of the Argentinian army behind them, every inch of the way.

Another attack came from the Argentine soldiers, now with the two GPMG machines on each Land Rover manned and working giving four guns in use the SAS manage to put down a heavy suppressing fire against the Argentinians, but the SAS men knew they could not hold here for too long as they would eventually be cut off and will run short of ammunition, so Colonel Bradley called all his men to get onto the Land Rovers, and then they would make a break for it, and head west towards the border with Chile, and as soon as the men were onboard they came under fire from the Argentinians again, but this time the SAS men put down a suppressing fire from there GPMG machine guns, and with that fire keeping the Argentinian heads down, the two Land Rovers were started up and they were the out and driving west along the straight road where the two Hercules had landed.

As the men looked back behind them, they could see the head lights of the Argentine vehicles, and as they expected the Argentinians were now on the road and behind them. The two Land Rovers drove down the straight road and passed the SAS Land Rovers that were left at the side of the road when the others got onto the Hercules.

*

Meanwhile the two Hercules were now moving back towards the west over towards the border with Chile, (if they were intercepted by any Argentine aircraft, then the two Hercules would turn and head over into Chile), and then back on route south towards there turning points that they followed when they arrived in Argentina, they were again at very low level, the mood onboard was not euphoric as they had two men down and one man wounded and on top of that ten men were left behind to fight.

Again, the men are finding that the ride onboard was bumpy as before, as the Hercules aircraft were bumping around in the turbulent air. The threat of any interceptor aircraft coming after them had now been put to the back of there minds as they could not think of any other airbases down here but on the same note, they were still cautious just in case, they were almost confident that nothing was left at Rio Grande airbase that could be launched, but there was enough time for aircraft from the bases to the north to have been scrabbled and launched.

Once they had reached the lakes that they used as a reference turning point when they arrived, they again turned, and then headed east out towards the Ocean. The ride was still bumpy and buffeting the aircraft around, again the brown paper bags were out with some of the men feeling sick from the turbulent ride. The wounded trooper was being checked over in the rear of Omen Two and his wound was not thought to be life threatening, if it had of been life threatening then Omen Two would have radioed on to the fleet, and they would have made an attempt to parachute the man with a couple of others so that they could get the wounded man onboard a ship to receive urgent medical treatment, but as luck will have it they will be able to return to Accession with him as he seems stable.

They are now heading towards Cabo San Pablo the small coastal town, and once past they will head out over the Ocean again for about twenty minutes, before they then head up to their cruising hight for their first refuel.

The two Hercules keep low and fly just over the Ocean as low as they would possibly dare, in the complete darkness, even above them the sky is blotted out by thick cloud, the two aircraft buffet their way through the turbulent air over the wild south Atlantic Ocean and then keep going for the twenty minutes that they had planned.

The pilots of both the Omen flights, were in contact with each other all the time planning the next stage and beyond. At two hundred Kilometres east of Cabo San Pablo, over the south Atlantic Ocean, the two Hercules start to make there climb up to a high altitude so that they could now cruise south of the Falkland Islands, and then turn and head north towards the first refuel point and then on towards their second refuel and then Accension island.

As they pass south of the Falkland islands, and then start to head north they revived a surprise visit, two Sea Harriers from the fleet that were on a late night combat air patrol had closed in next to the two Hercules to escort them for fifteen minutes as they headed nearer towards the fleet. This gave the two crews of the Hercules a warm feeling that they were now in safe hands with the Harriers there to protect them.

*

Back on the ground the two SAS Land Rover had reached the spot where the other SAS vehicles had been abandoned on the side of the road where the two Hercules had stood, they slowed down and with the 203 grenade launchers they launched a number of high explosive grenades into the vehicles, just to make sure that the Argentinians were not left any decent vehicles as a free gift by the Regiment.

They then put there foot down and speeded back up but had the Argentine soldiers starting to close up on them a little bit more. They came to the sharp bends just before they entered Estancia Maria Behety and raced through the small hamlet sliding the Land Rovers on the lose ground as they turned a long bend and the men were now having to grip onto anything inside the Land Rover to hang onto, as they entered the hamlet.

Sergeant Major Owen was driving the lead Land rover, and with him were Colonel Bradley, Chack, Major Austin and trooper Micky Watkins.

Following close behind them in the second Land Rover were Sergeant Billy Ballantine who was driving, Captain Rasheed, Corporal Jimmy Edwards, Sergeant Williams and Staff sergeant Paddy Kelly, everyone of these men had Years of experience with the SAS Regiment and all held an immense group of skills.

They powered out of the hamlet and back into the void countryside using there night vision goggles to see where they were going and to avoid using the lights on the Land Rovers, every now and then there would be a "zip" from a round that would be fired by one of the Argentinians in the perusing vehicles. Major Bradley was getting a bit concerned because the road was starting to head north west, and that would mean that the distance towards the border would have expanded, his eyes were glued too the road looking into the distance for an opportunity to maybe turn off and head north again or even for a shootout with the Argentinians that were in close pursuit, they were now ten kilometres along the road, and they were still going north west, Colonel Bradley was on the radio back to Captain Rasheed, they were now making plans, the road did not seem to be taking them into any kind of cover, and they were getting no nearer towards the border.

Colonel Bradley had decided to give it another five minutes, and then they will have to do something, then just as the five minutes had clicked the road started to head west around a long bend.

The SAS men turned and were heading west, they had just passed another large cattle ranch on there left, Colonel Bradley strained his eyes slightly as he could see what looked like some hills in the distance. The Argentine vehicles were still close behind them, there was no way that they could out run them to the border, the line had to be drawn in the sand and Colonel Bradley had now decided that they will have to fight now rather than later.

'Stand by chaps, we are going to stop in a moment and give the Argies a bit of a scrap,' he said to the men, he then radioed a message to Captain Rasheed, and told him that they will have to face the Argentinians.

The SAS Land Rovers slowed up a little bit, and the number two Land Rover pulled along side the lead Land Rover, they then slowed up, and then suddenly came to a complete halt in the road, and then turned with the side of the Land Rovers across the road blocking it.

Sergeant Major Owen and Chack, jumped up in the first Land Rover to take control of their two GPMG guns, and at the same time Rasheed and Billy Ballantine took control of the two GPMG guns in the second Land Rover, with Colonel Bradley and Major Austin acting as number two gunners feeding in the ammunition on the first Land Rover guns and Jimmy Edwards and Paddy Kelly as number twos on the second Land Rover.

The SAS men had now put down a fierce barrage of fire onto the first of the Argentine vehicles as it approached them, four GPMG machine guns were firing six to eight rounds in an accurate burst into the Argentinian pursuit vehicles, the first two ran off the road while they were peppered with 7.62 rounds, The SAS men on the GPMG's showed no mercy as they kept up an immense barrage of fire, the remaining two SAS men were busy firing round after round of 203 grenades into the pursuing vehicles, there were now large explosions, and any Argentine man who was trying to escape the fire was then quickly cut down by the SAS, GPMG,s Four Argentine vehicles were now hit, and now in flames, the SAS men were now firing and watching for muzzle flash from the Argentinians so that they could concentrate there fire on the Argentinians who were shooting back at them.

'Okay Boys lets go,' Colonel Bradley shouted out and as fast as they had stopped for the fight the SAS men were back down in their Land Rovers and hanging on again, and on their way again.

'That should have bought us some time,' Colonel Bradley shouted out.

The Land Rovers continued their drive looking for the border, but with the pursuing vehicles now destroyed they could relax just a little, and keep their eyes open for the border.

CHAPTER ELEVEN.

02.50.

The SAS men had now come into a wide open area with what they could see were hills all around, from what they could see it almost looked like the tops of the rolling mountains of Wales, they slowed down a little to try and see how far away from the border they were, the Magellan reading that they were getting, seemed to place them around fifteen kilometres away from the border with Chile, but with no detailed map to place the coordinates onto it was difficult to be accurate, all they had were coordinates that were given too them before the mission so a lot of their navigation was guesswork. But now the road that they have been on has come to what looked like an end.

The Land Rovers have pulled up at a white fenced area and it looked like the road had ended here, and the land was now private, it looked like the land from here was a ranch.

'What do you think Colonel,' Sergeant Major Owen said as they looked on at the fence.

'I don't now sergeant Major, but it looks like our only way to the border is by going along this road, we will have to risk it.'

There was now a noise somewhere above them that they all recognised and could pin point just south of them, the noise was the sound of helicopters. 'Well, it looks like we are going to have company, Colonel Bradly said as everyone looked over towards the area of the sound.

'I say we go ahead,' Sergeant Major Owen said.

'Well, we cannot go back that is for sure,' Colonel Bradley replied.

'I think we will have to fight for the border,'

Colonel Bradley listened to the sergeant major and then got out of the Land Rover and walked to the second one, 'have you all got ammo', Colonel Bradley asked. The men went through there pouches and presented mags full of ammunition, they had been given all the spare ammo from the SAS men that had left and headed towards the two Hercules .

'Okay men, we may have to fight for the border up ahead, it looks like the Argies have started to build up ready for our arrival,'

'Don't worry sir we will not go hard on them,' Billy Ballantine shouted over.

The Colonel put a large smile on his face when he heard the comment 'well don't go too soft with them Billy,' he replied.

'Don't you worry Sir, I will leave Mr Sykes in his pocket,' Colonel Bradley was happy his men had a high morale and still giving out some banter, and he then returned to his Land Rover, and then checked with the men in his Land Rover, too see if they had enough ammo, once he was happy that everyone had enough ammunition he climbed into his seat and the two SAS Land Rovers moved forward, through the white fenced area and then along the road.

The Land rovers moved along the road a little slower than they had been going, and then came to another small hamlet that was nestled within some small hills, this hamlet was called Castillo, and here lay another large working ranch, Estancia San Julio.

The Land Rovers moved along the road and had now come to a junction, one road went north while the other went south, the Land Rovers stopped, and Colonel Bradley had to decide which way to go.

'I only wish we had a bloody map,' Colonel Bradley said as he looked at each road. Take the road to the north and we will see if we can near the border that way. They drove along the road north and then around a long bend that went around one of the larger hills, they were now heading west again, and the Colonel was happy that they were back on course and near to the border, but as the road started to strengthen out, they could see about three helicopters just above the ground in the area to the west with headlights also on the ground, where they would have expected to see the border, the Land Rovers pulled up again.

'It looks like they are dropping of troops up their sir,' Sergeant Major Owen said as they all looked on.

'Shit, that has buggered the plan up, okay let us turn around and head down the other road that went south,' Colonel Bradley answered.

The two Land Rovers turned around and then headed back around the bend towards Castillo, they had all hoped that they would not bump into any Argentinians coming the other way.

As they came back into Castillo, and the working ranch, they looked back down the road they had come up along from Rio Grande and they could see bright lights in the distance heading their way. 'It looks like the Argentine army are on the way by road as well,' Colonel Bradley said as he looked on 'okay then forward we go,' he ordered.

The Land Rovers headed south and into a hillier area, 'Ahh, now this is more like our kind of landscape,' the Colonel said as he looked at the hills. The Land Rovers moved slowly forward.

*

The Two Hercules aircraft were now approaching there first refuelling point with a Victor tanker, again this was a vital task that they had to do, there current fuel level was now extremely low as they had to work with a minimum of fuel in order to land and take off from Rio Grande.

The pilots on the return journey were now the reserve crew that were taken on the flight, this meant that the aircraft were now being flown by a refreshed crew, and not a fatigued crew.

This was, this crews first refuel on this mission, and Omen One had now positioned itself behind the Victor tanker that was in a shallow dive, and the Hercules was now following it, and again with the aid of a torch and looking through the windscreen into the balk night sky, the Hercules crew had now successfully connected up to the basket and were now taking on vital fuel to get them to the next tanker that will top them up again later with enough fuel to continue their journey.

Once Omen One had refuelled, it would break off and Omen Two would then take in the same task, again with afresh pilot and crew they will refuel and then go on towards the second refuelling point for a top up to bring them home.

Meanwhile inside the Cargo hold of Omen One the men were doing what all SAS men do on a long flight, and that was to grab as much sleep as possible, the turbulence that they had experienced during the low flight had now gone and the two Hercules were cruising in the air without hardly any tremor at all. The war on the Falklands had not even begun to intensify as yet, and the men knew that as soon as they stepped off the Hercules back on accession then they would be back on board another one again and heading back towards the south Atlantic and either back onto a ship or direct onto the Islands, wherever they will go there job will not be finished until the war was over, so the more sleep they get now the better as their work load will increase again in the next few days.

Omen Two was now refuelled and the two Hercules were now flying side by side and heading north with the Victor Tanker just in front of them.

*

Back in Northwood there was still tension in the ops room, the Director had now left the building as he has now been called to another meeting with the Ministers, as there is now a lot of Diplomatic pressure building form Argentina and some of the countries that support her, even France has now called on the United Kingdom to explain why they have invaded a Sovereign Country.

With all this going on The Prime Minister has been in close talks with President Pinochet, and she needs to keep him on her side as the Director has now informed her that ten SAS men have made a run towards the border, and they will be crossing over into Chile, there is also the threat that Argentine troops will enter Chile in pursuit as they had already threatened to do so if there was a raid on any Argentine bases, and if any of the escaping British soldiers had crossed the border into Chile.

President Pinochet was as welcoming as he was before and was willing to help as much as he could, knowing that after all of this there would be some nice trade deals on the table with the united Kingdom and even Military equipment as well.

Colonel Cedric was busy listening out for any radio reports, he had just been given the message that the two Hercules had just had there first refuel, but as up to now he has not heard anything from the ten men that were left behind on the ground inside of Argentina.

All the team were listening in just in case they receive a message, Colonel Cedric was also aware that the ten men may not be in a position to make a radio update either because they were being pursued or they may want to remain in complete radio silence.

Colonel Thomas was also in the room, but he was now talking with Hereford just in case there were some other updates coming in from there. Also, GCHQ were keeping an ear on any radio messages that the Argentinians had been sending to see if they could pick up on any information, but so far nothing has come through.

*

Meanwhile Colonel Bradley and his men had come to a halt, there were more helicopter movements they could see west of their current position.

'I think they are putting men all along the border,' Colonel Bradley said as the men looked on at the helicopters that were flying in and out in the west, and what must have been along the border fence with Chile.

'How much fuel do we have Sergeant Major,' Colonel Bradley asked.

'Just over a half tank sir, and there are two Jerry cans on the back as well.'

'Okay, I say we head down this road, if it keeps going south, we should stay near the border as we go along, I think we need to see if the border is a bit clearer of Argentine soldiers to the south and go for it down there' the Colonel took a deep breath and looked around 'I say the border is a bit too crowded up here at the moment to try anything.'

The SAS Land Rovers now headed south along a narrow road, they still remained in an area with hills, but then it started to level out again and the large hills started to shrink down to flat ground once more. After a few more kilometres, the road they were on had now changed to what was more like a farm track, it was narrow and now more uneven, and the Land Rovers were now starting to rock from side to side and throw the men around more as they navigated their way along the road.

There were still helicopters flying low up and down the border that was now just five or more kilometres away from their position, there fear now was being sighted by a helicopter with its crew using night vision equipment, that may well be armed with air to ground rockets, as they have already found out the Argentinians have a

OPERATION MIKADO

good supply of quality night vison, so they could be spotted easy enough.

The road that they are following was heading south, south east , so was actually heading slowly towards the border, so the men were getting nearer, Colonel Bradley checked his watch it was 04.10, they had been driving around for ages, the longer they put anything off the harder it will be too cross the border, and he knew that the Argentinians would have realised by now that the SAS men had turned off and headed away from the junction at Castillo so he knew they would be looking for them along different routes and this one was a prime route.

'Okay hold up Sergeant Major,'

Sergeant Major Owen pulled up and the Land Rover behind stopped just behind them.

'I think it is time to dump the vehicles and make for the border on foot,' Colonel Bradley said as he climbed out of the Land Rover and looked around.

Captain Rasheed had come forward from his Land Rover too see what was happening 'Colonel,'

'Ah Khan, I think we should dump the vehicles and then make a run for the border, and then see if we can take our chances, and then cross over here, looking at the time it is starting to creep on, and it will start to go against us soon.'

Captain Rasheed looked around there were helicopters in the distances at the moment, and getting over the border would be a priority, 'I agree

Colonel, I think that we should go for the border, just here as well.'

'Major Austin, what do you say,'

'I say make a run for it, get over the border and go.'

'Okay' let us dump the Rovers, and make our way over the border on foot, we still may have to fight when we get there.' The men looked around at the flat ground they have found themselves in, there was very little in the way of cover. There was however an area that looked like it was small trees or large shrubs, this would be great for driving the Land Rovers into, and hiding them while the men make their way on foot.

'Okay everyone grab your kit from the Land Rovers, and we will drive them across here, and into that area of what looks like a scrub area,' Colonel Bradley said as he was pointing out to the men as they all turned and grabbed weapons and their small escape bergens from the Land Rovers.

They drove the Land Rovers slowly over the soft ground towards the shrubs one man in each Land Rover drove while the rest of the men ran along side ready to give covering fire. They moved across the soft land for four hundred metres until they reached the shrubs that were growing in a large area, and then drove the two Land Rovers into them, they then covered the Land Rovers with large camo nets to hide them.

With the Land Rovers covered the men were now all ready to move towards the border.

'Do you want us to put a few mines around the Land Rovers,' Sergeant Major Owen asked Colonel Bradley.

The Colonel stood in thought for a few moments before he answered, 'no, we best not, just in case some civilians discover the vehicles at a later date.'

'Right, you are then Sir, they are all covered and hidden away.'

'Thank you, Sergeant Major.'

Chack, was caught out by the events of the evening, his large bergen was slung into the Hercules before the mission set off towards the airbase, so that he could travel light and lead everyone in, however now he has no kit other than ammunition because the two Hercs left before he could retain his bergen.

'So, you have no rations or anything,' Sergeant Major Owen asked him.

'No nothing, it al went into the Herc.'

'Well don't worry lad, we will sort something out once we get over the border, hopefully we will get picked up quick as well on the other side.'

All the men were now ready to move towards the border, Captain Rasheed had taken a little walk south and found that there was a river running east to west about a kilometre away from their position.

'Just down their Colonel, it looks a large river,' Rasheed commented.

'Interesting, I do know that some reports have said we will have to go over a fence so maybe the river was clear of any fences,' Colonel Bradley thought for a moment before he continued, 'I tell you what, I think we should go that way and see if we can cross into Chile along the river.'

The SAS men moved into a single file and moved along slowly towards the river, sergeant Williams took point, and he led the men slowly forward, towards the river, it did not take the men long to reach the river bank, the river was in a very large flood plain, it looked as though the river flooded often and when it did it covered a vast amount of land. The men halted and went down into a prone position while Colonel Bradley looked at the situation with his officers.

Once they were happy, they now started to move forward towards the border. They were about five kilometres away from the border, they were so close to it, and they were now confident that they could just slip over too the other side and disappear into Chile.

It was Sergeant Ballantine that first see the indication that something was up ahead of them, Sergeant Ballantine noticed a small glowing light up front, he passed on through the SAS men to stop and they all dropped down into a prone position giving an all around defence, at the same time Sergeant Ballantine looked through his night vision at the area that he see the glow, and then he could see what was making the glow, a Argentine soldier was stood next to a vehicle smoking a cigarette, the lighted end could be seen even though the Argentine soldier had tried to keep the cigarette covered with his hands.

Sergeant Ballantine then moved himself around a little to try and see what was around and then he could see a large gathering of vehicles just up ahead, and on both sides of the river.

'There must be around a hundred men just up there,' he whispered.

'Are they in just one area,' Sergeant Major Owen asked.

'No, they are spread out a bit but not very far from each other, they have night vision on there weapons, and there is way too many for us to handle in one rush.'

Sergeant Major Owen passed the information on to Colonel Owen. 'Damn it, we will have to look elsewhere.'

'North or south, sir,' Sergeant Major Owen asked.

'I think we will have to head back up north a little and have a look at what we can find.'

The SAS men moved back out and headed north, they were now even more cautious just in case there were any enemy patrols out. There were a few raised areas that they could see so these would give them some cover as they moved back up north, another thing that they had now noticed was that to the west there were what looked like trees growing, these would give the men some more cover so the SAS men now moved towards the trees, the trees will give them excellent cover.

It was hard to tell what type of trees were growing here, so far, the men had not seen any trees only grass and flat land, with lakes and marshes and the occasional river running through. Tree cover will give the men excellent cover and will help them maybe get closer towards the border.

As they walk into the wooded area, they are greeted with the unusual sight of trees that seem to have been flattened off at the top, this flattened off has been created by the winds that are constantly blowing across the region. With the flat top the tree continues to grow sideways and almost look like they are blowing like a flag in the wind.

The land here is also raised in areas, but the raised areas have no trees growing so the men keep on the lower part, the trees have now delt the SAS men an upper hand, this is their kind of land, the type of land that they carry out a vast amount of there training in and a type of land where they will use it to their advantage.

CHAPTER TWELVE.

London.

It was a bright sunny morning in London and the Prime Minister herself, was now being briefed on the latest developments down in the south Atlantic, there was a large amount of information to be looked at each morning, and these daily meetings had taken up a lot of time, but the top of the agenda was the overnight mission that destroyed the aircraft and four Exocet missiles at Rio Grande airbase.

Amongst the Ministers at the meeting was also the Director of Special Forces, who would now have to give the Prime Minister an up to date account of what had happened during the night time raid, and also the current situation on the ground in Argentina, where the ten SAS men were still inside, and also that up to now no news had been received from the men.

The Prime Minister had sat quite and patiently while the Director went through everything that they know so far, as the prime Minister listened, she slowly nodded her head in agreement to the Director as he went through all known details, the Prime Minister herself was a thorough listener, and she would listen carefully, and take in every detail that was now being said.

When the Director had finished, one of the Ministers took the opportunity to ask the Prime Minister 'when will you make an announcement to the press,' she put her had up to halt him in his tracks, and then turned sharply and looked at all her Ministers 'no one will be making any announcement to any press, not until those ten men are safe, and over the border inside of Chile, and out of harm's way ' she then stopped and looked around the table as she continued, her steel stare was now seeking out anyone that may dare to go against her wishes, 'do I make myself clear,' she continued in a raised voice and a slight movement of her head.

There were mutterings from all around the table as he Ministers agreed with what she had just said. Her gaze remained on each Minister before she continued, and again addressed the Director, 'now Brigadier General, I believe there have been two fatalities and one wounded, am I correct.'

'Yes Mam, you are correct.'

The Prime Minister sat silent for a moment before she continued her mind was busy thinking of the current situation,

'I will meet with the Chilean ambassador

later today, I will seek a guarantee that if the men get over the border, and into Chile, then they will be protected and hurried through and back out of the country. And I do not wish to have any more casualties.'

'Thank you, Mam,'

'Now let us move onto the other details of the day.'

This was the point when the Director would excuse himself, and then return to Northwood to gain the latest updates, he was happy with the Prime Ministers fullest support for his men and their Mission.

*

Major Castillo was annoyed that he had lost two of his best men trying to stop the SAS from escaping from the airbase, he was even more annoyed when he had learnt that another four men had been lost in an ambush on the road towards the border with Chile, as they were in pursuit of the SAS men.

He was now at the border fence, near to Estancia El Salvador a large ranch that ran along the border with Chile. Major Castillo had flown in with a few of his men by helicopter and were now awaiting the arrival of the SAS men at some point along the border, but so far there was no indication of them, and now some foot patrols had been sent out to look for any signs of the men.

There had been a few hundred men now transported up to the border at various locations where they expected the SAS men to cross over, and they were now convinced that they had this part of the border secured, they only had a few hours left before daylight would start to appear, and with very little cover the SAS men would be exposed and captured.

The Major kept his men ready he knew that the SAS men would just appear, and they would be fast, and they would attempt to run through the border, but he had also been given orders to pursue the men into Chile if necessary to capture them and bring them back to Argentina. The Junta knew how valuable the men would be to them if they were captured.

Argentine soldiers were now spaced out along the border fence, the fence itself was low just six feet high, and there was one fence running along the Argentine border, and one along the Chilean border that was identical with a six foot gap between the fences, so any men who would escape would have to climb two fences.

*

As the SAS men are now making a reconnaissance watch of the fence in front of them, they can now see, just how well it is now being guarded. The Argentinians know that they will have to escape over the border, and they know from the pursuit that they would have to cross over in this area so they have now pushed as many men up here as they could get a hold off.

The Argentinians also have a barracks at a

border crossing south of here at Bella Vista, so they have cleared the men out and sent them up here to the border fence to keep watch along with units from the Marines and Buzos Tacticos, and other conscript Regiments that were nearby.

Colonel Bradley could see a large concentration of men again along here, 'well we have a choice, we can stay here and wait out, and hope that they will go away, or we can try and find a place to cross.'

'I say we get the Land Rovers back and head back up to the road we came on and head in towards the border up there,' Captain Rasheed answered,

'I think we stand a better chance up there as well,' Sergeant Major Owen added.

Colonel Bradley thought for moment before he answered, 'Okay let's get the Rovers back out and head back up there, maybe we may get a break up that way.'

The SAS men made there way back to the Land Rovers and uncovered them and then drove them back over to the narrow road they had come down, the men all climbed back into the Land Rovers, Colonel Bradley was worried about the time, but just as he was worried about the time the heavens opened and the rain came down. 'You lot are lucky,' said Chack, 'you have had a dry spell up to now.'

The rain poured down and made the drive a few miles north even more miserable as the wind and the wet seeped through each man, making him feel colder and wetter, Chack was a lot better off as he still had his Argentine army coat that he had stolen, and that was well made and waterproof and warm.

The two Land Rovers headed up the road and Colonel Bradley was starting to think that maybe they should split into two group, they may have a better chance of escaping if they did so.

They finally reached the large ranch buildings at the village of Castillo; this area seemed a lot better as they had high hills around them as well. They rounded the corner and started to head slowly west towards the border, They travelled through an area that had a number of hills on each side of the road, and for some reason they took comfort from this kind of land around them, it was again almost like a Welsh mountain road.

Colonel Bradly looked at his watch it was gone five, 'what time does it get light here,' Colonel Bradley asked Chack as he turned in his seat to talk with him.

'About eight thirty and nine in the morning it starts to brighten.'

'Damn we are running short on time; we need to get this crossing done no matter what.'

The rain was still heavy as they came through the last valley formation and could see now that the land had started to flatten again and open up again as it went towards the border.

'Damn this place,' Colonel Bradley said out

loud.

The SAS men in the Land Rovers had to pass yet another ranch and they could now see that the people of this ranch were now waking up and starting there busy day as lights were on in the big buildings and the small houses. Just opposite the ranch Colonel Bradley could see a hill with a track leading towards it, 'turn here,' he pointed towards the track and Sergeant Major Owen made a right hand turn onto a narrow track. and then followed it slowly with the other Land Rover just behind him.

They moved up the hill towards the top. On the right hand side, they had a cattle fence that would keep the cattle inside that area, and on there left it was open, they entered a small valley that ran into the hill, it was not steep, but it was getting a little slippery as the Land Rovers were struggling for grip on the wet grass and the mud and lose stones, but being careful and keeping the engines at low revs so that they did not make too much noise they slowly headed towards the top of the hill.

The hill was a lot higher than they had thought it would be but once they were at the top they could drive along with ease towards the west. They then descended down into another set of small hills and found another valley to move along so they were almost a few kilometres from the border fence. They stopped and looked forward and could see a group of trees on the Argentine side of the border and the same group of trees thickened out on the Chilian side of the border.

'Okay men we will have to make this our last chance, the concentration of men down there does not look as thick as it was at the other points, we have just got that damn fence to deal with,' Colonel Bradley said.

Billy Ballantine was rooting about in the back of the one Land Rover, 'Aye don't forget we still have these,' he said as he pulled out a Milan launcher and two missiles in there carry tubes, all ready too fit to the launcher.

'Well done, do we have a night vision converter for that launcher,' Colonel Bradley asked.

'Aye, boss we certainly do.'

'Splendid, we could in theory blast a hole in that fence, unless we use a Land Rover to crash though.'

'The only problem we have with the Land Rover, boss is the fact that the fence has the posts tight together, that indicates that the fence is well secured and even a Land Rover will struggle to burst through,' Sergeant Major Owen replied.

'Okay then, we could use the Milan to blow a hole into the fence and then we would have to run through the gap,'

'Yes boss, it looks like we will have to do that.'

'Okay then so we will still have to fight our way through, so we will need some kind of plan of action drawn up,' the Colonel replied.

The men had no map of the area, no maps were ever made available, the land here was anyone's guess to what it would be looking like, so any plan would have to be done with a visual sighting of the fence, and the position of the Argentine troops along the border fence and for that they would have to move in even closer to the border, any action would have to be fast. Again, the Land Rovers would have to be left where they are, as they could not risk trying to get them through the fence and take them with them is case, they get stuck.

Colonel Bradley called the men around, for a chin wag and to see if they could come up with some kind of plan. The men circle around but they remain ready with there weapons just in case anyone walks in on their position.

'Okay men we need to go through the fence, we have the Land Rovers and the Milan, any ideas,' Colonel Bradley asked.

'We could barge through with the Land Rovers,' Sergeant Kelly suggested.

'No, the fence is secured with two many fences, it was put up to stop any vehicle from getting through,' Captain Rasheed replied.

'Hit the fence roots with a Milan, that should blow a hole wide enough to get us through on foot,' Micky Watkins replied.

'Well so far the Milan seems to be our best option,' Colonel Bradley added.

'If you hit it with the Milan then we could

then use the confusion of the missile blast to launch an attack on the Argies in that area,' Chack added.

'We need to move a lot closer than we are now,' Billy Ballantine added.

Colonel Bradley placed his hand up by his face with his palm outwards, 'okay it looks like we are in with the Milan, I think we should move closer and leave the Land Rovers here.

'Do you want me to booby trap the Land Rovers boss,' Jimmy Edwards asked.

'No, I think we better leave the Land Rovers in working condition just in case the plan goes pear shaped, at least we will still have them to fall back on if we need to escape.'

'Okay lads grab what you can, we will be on shanks pony from here on,' Sergeant Major Owen said to the men.

The men stripped off the GPMG machine guns from there mountings the four GPMG machine guns can be used in a fire fight to escape and would put down an immense fire onto the enemy, they still have plenty of 7.62 ammunition for the four machine guns as well as their CAR 15 assault rifles and the MP5SD silenced weapons as well as some grenades, 203 grenades and launchers and two Milan missiles, They also have a few LAW 66 mm light anti-tank weapons as well.

With their weapon and ammunition load the men now make there way slowly down the hill and towards some trees that they had spotted that are in front of the border fence. They picked the area with the trees because on the other side of the border inside of Chile, the trees are much more, denser at the same spot, so if they crossed the border here, they would be under cover quickly.

The men start to move out keeping low to the ground and moving slowly, as they do not want to draw attention to themselves, at the moment the men have there MP5SD sub machineguns at the ready, just in case some one walks in front of them at least they can respond in some silence.

Although the land is flat, there is enough undulation to create some small shallow valleys that are ideal to give the men cover as they make there way forward. They had moved along for about three kilometres and were now on the edge of the trees that were growing on the Argentine side of the border, these trees did not give them too much cover but were enough to help them.

They now had less that one kilometre to go, they were now in a thicker part of the trees and were working there way slowly forward, they could hear voices just in front of them and the SAS men went prone onto the ground, and then they looked in front of their position to see who was talking.

They spotted three Argentine soldiers, who were down behind a machine gun, Billy Ballantine and Micky Watkins made themselves ready, and then they snake crawled forward keeping low and under cover as they moved. The machine gun was about twenty metres away, so they had a good distance to crawl. They moved out to the right of the machine gun position, and then crawled over behind the position and then slowly moved forward towards it.

The three Argentine soldiers were chatting and laughing, and one was even hiding a cigarette and smoking, but they were totally unaware of the two SAS men that were now creeping up on them from behind. as the three Argentines lay behind there GPMG in the pouring rain inside the wooded area, they were totally unaware that two SAS men had stood up just behind them and had now moved there MP5SD sub machine guns into their shoulders ready to fire.

The three Argentine soldiers laughed their final laugh and drew their final draw of cigarette smoke, and were then hit with the silence of three or four rounds into there backs, each man was dead before his head rested onto the ground.

The three Argentine soldiers lay face down with just a feint cloud of smoke rising up from there wounds, one of them was still jerking as his nervous system was closing down.

The two SAS men walked forward keeping their weapons on the men as they checked that they were dead and no longer a threat. Billy Ballantine unloaded there GPMG and picked up all their belts of 7.62 ammunition, it will be all useful for the SAS men when they make there attack on the border fence.

Colonel Bradley had taken the opportunity to send out a message, he knew that there were SAS teams inside of Chile, and he was in hope that some men would turn up on the other side of the border to pick them up. His message will also be sent onwards to Northwood to let them know that the ten man team were still inside of Argentina, and they were trying to get over the border.

It was now 05.40 time was going against them, they would have to launch their attack on the border fence before daybreak, it was still raining but had eased off a little so not so heavy, each man was now cold and wet, they need to move as soon as possible.

The men now moved forward, Billy Ballantine had shared out the Argentine 7.62 ammunition, so each GPMG now had extra ammunition. They were now halfway through the wooded area, and now they had a clear view towards the fence and could now also see the shadows of the Argentine solders walking up and down trying to keep warm as they continued their guard on the border.

'Have you got a straight clear shot of the fence, with the Milan,' Colonel Bradley asked Billy Ballantine.

'Aye, boss, we can see the fence and have nothing in the way, I say we put both missiles in there and make sure the fence is blown before we move forward.'

'Okay, can you reload fast enough.'

'Aye, boss, me and Micky here are the best,

we will load and fire two missiles in that fence before you can blink.'

'Okay I will get the gun groups forward with the GPMG machine guns, two to the left and two to the right, as soon as you hit the fence, we will put down a barrage of fire onto the Argentine soldiers guarding the fence, and once we have made it a bit more clear we will go for the fence.'

Colonel Bradley went about his men and gave them a quick rundown of a plan, it was strange, but the gun teams would take up the eight men and the two on the Milan will take up the entire ten men, so as soon as they have laid down the missiles, and the machine gun fire, they will have to run like anything towards the border fence.

Within the small wood that they found themselves in they had a good amount of cover, this was the ideal spot for them, and now they had moved forward into their positions, and all had made themselves ready.

The GPMGs will be used to give accurate fire onto the Argentinian soldiers, they had enough ammunition to conflict heavy casualties onto the Argentinians, and to also give themselves plenty of time to run the two hundred meters to the fence.

Everyone was ready the GPMGs were fed with a belt of 7.62 round the cocking handle pulled back and the weapon ready to fire, the men had now secured the MP5SD sub machine guns to there backs and the CAR 15 were now placed so that they could use them as soon as they had finished with the GPMG.

The order was as soon as the first Milan hits the fence then they give the Argentinians some shit with the GPMG, all the men lay in wait they all had picked out their spaces and had picked out their arc of fire onto the Argentine soldiers along the fence, the GPMG will give them plenty of distance for there killing zones, with there night vision googles they now watched their targets.

"Whooosh", the first Milan went down through the trees and hit the fence with a large explosion, and at that the four GPMG machine guns opened up on the unsuspecting Argentine soldiers, the only sound other than the machine guns firing was the sound of men screaming as they were being cut down by the 7.62 rounds from the four GPMG machine guns. There was another "Whoosh", as the second Milan missile hit the border fence on the Chilian side of the border, the explosion had blow the fence and the fence posts into the air, and any Argentine soldier that was around the target are was also hit.

The SAS men were putting down eight to ten round bursts onto the Argentine positions, they had belts of 80 rounds feeding into the machine guns and were quickly having to do lightning reloads of fresh belts of ammunition. As they fired the two SAS men who had fired the Milan had now abandoned the launcher and destroyed it with rifle fire, they were now running forward towards the fence to secure the area and put down covering fire with their CAR 15 assault rifles, they were now putting down accurate fire on anyone that was in the areas. They looked on as both areas that were being hit with the GPMG fire had rounds and tracers bouncing around through the sky.

The furthest pair of gun teams now got up and ran forward towards the border fence, and when they arrived, they got down and put down a barrage of fire into the Argentinian soldiers so that the other two GPMG gun teams could now move in towards the fence.

All men now moved through the fence and into the woodland, they were now inside of Chile. But the Argentinians were now moving along the border fence towards the hole and were now firing onto the SAS men, the feeling of relief that they had just got from crossing over the border had now vanished as the hard fact that the Argentinians were still putting down fire on them.

The SAS men moved slowly into the trees, the trees here had given them some good cover, the GPMG guns were now out of ammunition, but they had done their job, the SAS men quickly stripped the GPMG guns of the barrel and working parts so that the guns would be dropped to the ground now that the ammunition had all been used, but the Argentinians would not be able to use the GPMG against the SAS men if they come across them as the working parts had been removed.

The SAS men moved into the forest but were now being pursued by Argentine soldiers, the fighting had not ended here in fact it seemed to have intensified. The SAS men had now fired about a dozen 203 grenades towards the Argentine soldiers and now they seemed to have a slight respite in the fighting.

Colonel Bradley was trying to get a bearing but the illumination on his compass had now failed, they had moved about one hundred and fifty metres through the forest and had now come out onto a dirt road that run through the forest, as they came out they came out into the open part of the dirt road they came under fire from a group of soldiers further up the road that had also come out of the trees. The SAS men put down some fire on the soldiers and then dived into the trees on the other side of the dirt road.

Little did the SAS men know but Major Castillo had now joined the Argentine army along the fence with a company of Marines, they had arrived two kilometres to the south of where the SAS men had breached the border fence, and their orders were to eliminate the SAS men or capture them, even if it meant going over the border and then deep inside of Chile.

The SAS men had now run through a gap in the forest that they were in and were heading west, every now and then they would come under fire from Argentine soldiers that were now moving west but also trying to close in on the SAS men and this would mean that they would have to take cover, and this was slowing down their progress.

Colonel Bradley was now having to be thinking on his feet as they moved forward, they could all split and scatter, and then make a run for it, he thought. What he did not expect was that the Argentinians would cross over the border and pursue them into Chile, the Argentinians had in the past hinted that they would do this, but no one ever thought that they would actually cross the border, he was also thinking that maybe other SAS men that are inside of Chile may well turn up at some point and pick the men up.

They were now one kilometre inside of Chile and thankfully they were still inside a forest, they had closed in on each other and were now slowly moving as one, and giving an all around defence, ready to repel any attack from any side or front and rear, they moved slowly and carefully as they made their way through the forest in the darkness.

Colonel Bradley also knew that at anytime soon the sun will start to rise and there will be the start of daylight, and this would add to their problems.

Just as they reached another track that run through the forest they came under fire again, a small group of Argentine Marines had moved forward quickly and had set up an ambush on the track as they expected the SAS men to appear at any moment, there plan was to keep them there while the rest of the Argentine Marines had caught up with them.

Springing an ambush upon a team of SAS

men was one thing, but actually stopping the SAS men when they went through there anti ambush drills was something else, the SAS men dropped into there fighting positions, and with the use of 203 grenades and an intense barrage of fire, they were quickly over the track, and into the group of Argentine Marines that had set up the ambush. They ran through the Marines leaving only two men alive.

The SAS men moved quick back into the forest and were again heading west, again they were receiving single incoming rounds from the Argentinians who were not that far behind them.

A group of the Argentine Marines had taken advantage of running around the outskirts of the forest, they knew that if they ran along the edge, they would overtake anyone travelling through the forest, and that there were also a number of tracks that went north to south through the forest so they could then turn and run along one of these tracks and hopefully cut the SAS men off.

Major Castillo had taken fifteen men along this route and he was determined to stop the SAS men from going any further into Chile, he also knew that at some point the Chilian army would turn up once the civilian people in the area started to hear the intense gun fire, so the clock was ticking, he had to stop them as fast as he could.

CHAPTER THIRTEEN.

Stokesey and a group of SAS men were inside Chile and had been in Punta Arenas and had been carrying out missions from there base in the city into mainland Argentina, they were mainly covert reconnaissance missions. However, they had been informed a that an assault would be carried out at Rio Grande and that some SAS men may make for the border if the aircraft that carried them into Argentina had been destroyed during their mission.

Stokesey, along with himself, had made up a ten man team, and had now moved through Chile over too a hide a few miles inside of Chile west of the Argentine border just in case the men from Mikado had to head over the border into Chile, they could then go in and extract any SAS team that made the run across the border.

They had just been informed that a ten man SAS team were coming through the border somewhere west of Rio Grande, however they had given there final Magellan position and that gave

Stokesey and his team an idea where the men would come across the border into Chile, so they left there hide and moved up into the area where they had expected Colonel Bradley and his team to appear.

Stokesey and his team were all heavily armed with CAR 15 assault rifles 203 grenade launchers and two GPMG machine guns, they moved up to a main road that ran north to south and parked up inside some tree cover at the side of the main road and then they all waited inside the forest for any sign of any soldiers coming through.

As always in this part of the World, there is a brisk wind that blows from the west so any sound from the east is deadened by the wind carrying the sound away and also the trees in the forest, so Stokesey and his men had a job hearing anything.

Stokesey double checked the last Magellan reading that was received from Colonel Bradley, and he also checked his current position, as long as Colonel Bradley and his men held a westerly approach, they would come out somewhere along this point.

The men kept on listening out just in case there was any shooting but then thought that maybe the Argentine threat was just what they said, a threat, and that they would not dare to cross the border into Chile in pursuit of any British troops.

Colonel Bradley and his men had stopped to take in the situation, they had to do an ammunition count to make sure that they had enough ammunition to be engaged into another fire fight, they also had there MP5SD weapons that they could use but were now very low on ammunition for these.

They were now down to about one hundred rounds each, but to put down a fierce firefight they would soon be through all of that ammunition.

'Okay men, if we come under fire, switch to well-aimed shots make the rounds count, we should be getting into a position soon where the Argentinians will have to halt this pursuit,' Colonel Bradley said as he looked on to each man.

The men could also hear the sound of breaking tree branches approaching them as they spoke. Billy Ballantine had sneaked around to have a look and then returned, 'There are about twenty of them coming towards us,' Billy reported.

'No way to avoid them then,' Colonel Bradley asked.

'No boss, they will be onto us at any moment.'

'Okay men we will ambush them here, make the rounds count and try and conserve the ammo.'

The men spread out around the trees and kept down low and waited for the Argentine troops to appear, they were not Argentine Marines, but they were conscripted Argentine soldiers, and as they approached they did so in a manner that showed that they must have had about one weeks basic military training. They were cracking branches under there feet, there kit was rattling, and some were even smoking, and others were just chatting, they never stood a chance, the sound of gunfire erupted before the Argentine soldiers knew what was happening, all of the Argentine soldiers dropped in the accurate fire that was rained upon them, only two men managed to dive down behind some trees, they then attempted to fire some aimed shots but were quickly hit with two 203 grenades, the last one standing, was now running back towards the east he had also abandoned his FN rifle as he ran.

The SAS men were fast as they moved over towards the bodies of the Argentinian soldiers to make sure they were no longer a danger to them, but they also took the opportunity to collected their weapons, the FN FAL 7.62 a similar weapon used by the British army (SLR), but with an option to use on full automatic fire as an assault weapon, each Argentine soldier had around twenty rounds on him, not a lot but it was twenty rounds that the SAS men could use in a fire fight, they also gained a GPMG with one hundred and twenty rounds, again a useful weapon that they could use in a fight.

The SAS men made there way forward again but there last firefight had now drawn another group of Argentine troops towards them, again they elected to fight the Argentine troops, these troops seemed to be led by an officer who thought that a cavalry charge would be the best way to launch his attack, there were ten men in this assault but as they charged forward the SAS men set the FN rifles to full automatic and with a burst of two to three rounds they quickly dispensed of the ten Argentine soldiers.

'Come on men,' Colonel Bradley shouted, he wanted to move his men along as fast as possible and try and get out of there current situation, it would only be a matter of time before they take a hit and that is one thing, he wanted to avoid at all costs.

The men moved on again on there western bearing, through the trees, there were now some areas where the grass had grown into tall yellow bunches and that offered the men some extra cover, the trees were also growing in a thicker formation through the forest.

They came upon another track that crossed their path, and as they slowed up and checked the track, they could see it looked all clear. Colonel Bradley also noticed that the sky was starting to look a little lighter, there was now the danger of daybreak making it brighter and exposing the men a little bit more.

As the men moved slowly towards the track ready to cross, they came under fire, they all jumped back into the cover of the trees, they used there night vision to check to see where the enemy position was but, the enemy were well hidden, they also came under fire as soon as they placed there heads out from the trees.

'Can anyone see anything', Colonel Bradley

asked.

'I could see some muzzle flash about one hundred metres along that track towards the south,' Billy Ballantine answered.

'And those are five, fifty six rounds not seven, sixty two,' Captain Rasheed answered.

'They must be Argentine Marines,' Sergeant Major Owen added. 'They are using M16 rifles.'

Colonel Bradley was looking around just trying to get a head count, he could see one man missing, 'everyone here,' he asked.

The men checked themselves out, there was one missing, 'Sergeant Williams is down boss,' someone answered.

'What do you mean down,' Colonel Bradley asked.

'He is down on the track, it looks like he has been hit a number of times, I do not think he is breathing boss,'

'Oh no,' Colonel Bradley said softly. The last thing that the Colonel wanted was any casualties.

Billy Ballantine had moved to the edge, he had his 203 grenade launcher at the ready, he popped in a red and gold grenade, a high explosive dual purpose grenade, he crept onto some of the thick grass and looked over to where he had last seen the muzzle flash, and now with a careful aim he squeezed the trigger, and with the muffled thump he launched a grenade over towards the area.

There was a loud explosion in between the

trees, the SAS men were ready to cross the track but as they moved forward, they came under fire again. 'Shit they are still in there,' Major Austin said as the men pulled back into the trees again.

*

Stokesey and his men were still at the edge of the forest near to the main road trying to listen out for any kind of noise, it was when the 203 grenade had gone off, did they finally get to hear something.

'Dead east,' one of the men shouted, and at that Stokesey and his men started to move slowly into the trees and head towards the east, in search of the Mikado team.

*

Colonel Bradley was checking his men's ammunition again to make sure that they had a sufficient level to carry on with the fight, they were all now well below one hundred rounds, so now they were running very low, Colonel Bradley had not imagined that the Argentinians would pursue them into Chile, although they had always threatened to do so.

Billy Ballantine moved over towards the Colonel, 'boss, I can hear movement to our east, I think we have company heading towards us.'

'That is all we need,' Colonel Bradley answered, 'keep your eye on the situation.

'Aye boss.'

Captain Rasheed had now moved forward to have a look at the area where the Marines are believed to be under cover, he had a 203 launcher and he has just loaded his launcher with a high explosive grenade and was now aiming at the general area of the Argentine Marines, he wanted to fire a grenade into them, and then see if there is any movement or muzzle fire that would give there position away, he kept looking and then fired the 203 sending a grenade into the trees where they suspected the Marines to be hiding under cover, there was an explosion and Rasheed and Major Austin watched ready to see where the muzzle flash would come from, but there was no return fire from the Argentine Marines.

'Maybe we have hit them all,' Major Austin said.

'No there in there, they just figured out what we were doing,' Captain Rasheed answered.

'We have that GPMG don't forget,' Major Austin said as he looked over to Captain Rasheed.

'It may well be worth putting some rounds in there then,' Captain Rasheed answered.

Captain Rasheed whispered out for the GPMG, and Paddy Kelly moved forward, 'What do you want' he asked as he moved forward with the GPMG.

'Have a look through your night vision, can you see about one hundred metres out along the path, there is a small tree that has been hit and has gone over,' Rasheed said to Paddy.

'Yeah, I can see it, cut a few feet from the ground and all jagged, is that the one.'

'Yes, that is the one, now if you go just past that tree about five feet, we think that someone is in there.'

Paddy was looking for a few minutes before he replied, 'I am not sure boss, but I think I have just seen someone in there, shall I drop a few rounds on them.'

'If you would.'

Paddy Pulled the cocking handle back and engaged the first round from a long belt of 7.62 rounds, Captain Rasheed moved in next to him to act as his number two on the gun, he had the bipod out ready and moved up toward the gun, he had good cover around himself as he looked on towards the area that he had picked out, he pulled the gun up into his shoulder and gently leaned it forward so that its memento was pressed against the bipod, and then he pushed the safety button over ready to fire, and carefully aimed with his normal eyesight towards the area he had seen with the night vision goggles. Paddy squeezed the trigger and sent a burst of eight rounds into the area that he had been looking at, two tracers had gone in to the area they had just started to glow as they reached the trees, Paddy then moved slightly to he left and put another burst of rounds into the area and then moved to his right and put another eight rounds in, a couple of tracers hit the area and bounced up through the trees bouncing around the forest.

The Argentine Marines fired back and gave

away their positions with their muzzle flash, Captain Rasheed and Major Austin quickly fired off a couple of high explosive 203 grenades into their positions, one of the grenades went off and was accompanied by a high pitched scream as one of the Marines was hit from the exploding grenade.

Paddy had stopped firing as he wanted to save as much ammunition as he could, just in case Colonel Bradley called for them to shoot their way across the track, at least with the GPMG they can put down some heavy fire, and keep the Argies heads down.

Billy Ballentine was back, 'There are some Argies about two hundred metres away heading towards our position boss.'

'Well, we will have to fight it out, I say we should engage them with the MP5s, and then we can keep the good ammo for the breakout through these Marines,' Sergeant Major Owen said.

'Okay then, we will need to keep an eye on those Marines because as soon as we engaged this lot coming in at us, those Marines will take the opportunity to come at us from behind,' Colonel Bradley was interrupted by a message that had been transmitted, he checked the message text. *'We will approach you from the west Bravo one, one, out.'*

'Well gents it looks like we will be getting company from the west, we have some of our men from the Regiment moving in towards us from the west, so let us take care of this lot coming towards us from the east.'

The SAS men got themselves ready with the MP5SD silenced sub machine guns and waited for the approaching Argentine forces that were coming through the forest towards them, meanwhile Captain Rasheed had three men with him watching the Marines at the rear ready to put down some fire upon them.

The men were all ready and waiting, as soon as the Argentine soldiers moved within fifty metres they opened fire with the MP5, s, they took the Argentinians by surprise as the silenced weapons ripped into the Argentine soldiers and they did not know what was happening, but a radio message from the Marines had now warned them where the SAS men's position was, and now they had all dived for cover behind the trees.

Captain Rasheed was waiting for the Argentine Marines to move forward but as yet they had not made there move, Rasheed was now thinking that the Marines have coordinated with the advancing Argentines and have now got them to move around towards the north and begin to circle around the SAS men's position in an attempt to stop them from escaping the area.

Captain Rasheed moved down towards Colonel Bradley. 'I think they are trying to surround us; I think they have men moving around to the north of us.'

'Right, we have another SAS team moving towards us from the west, I say we hit the Marines with everything and then dive across that track, and head towards the incoming team,' Colonel Bradley answered.

'I will take the body of Sergeant Williams as we make the run, I will carry him back with us,' Billy Ballentine said.

'I will place two Claymores just over there,' Chack said as he pointed in the direction of the advancing Argentine army.

'Okay men lets get going,' Colonel Bradley answered.

The men made ready Chack had set up the two Claymores with trip wires ready to slow up any advance from the Argentinians. The men all got ready, Billy Ballentine would grab Sergeant Williams as they crossed the track and throw him over his shoulder to carry his body with them.

'Ready then men, lets do it.' Colonel Bradley said as the men all ready with there CAR 15 rifles, they made a move at crossing the track, as soon as they appeared they came under fire, Billy Ballentine grabbed Sergeant Williams body and dragged it across the track, as he did so two or three rounds zipped past his head, Colonel Bradly was then hit In the leg as he ran across the track, although the men ran as fast as they could, Sergeant Major Owen had got hit in his back and Major Austin had taken a hit to the stomach and Captain Rasheed was hit by three rounds to his chest, Chack managed to grab Rasheed and pulled him over the track into the trees, but it was clear that his three wounds were fatal and Captain Rasheed passed away on the spot.

As soon as the SAS men had crossed into the trees the two Claymores had gone off sending seven hundred ball bearings from each mine thundering out towards the Argentinian soldiers.

'That will be the Claymores,' Billy Ballantine said with a laugh.

No one knew if they had hit any of the Marines, they had now expended most of their ammunition and the GPMG they had was completely out so they stripped that and threw the parts into the trees so that it could not be used, they now had two dead to carry with them and three wounded men as they tried to make their way through the forest.

The Argentine Marines were now moving with them and keeping a rain of fire on the SAS men as they tried to slowly move through the forest, the Marines knew that they had wounded the men and were now advancing to finish them off. Colonel Bradley shouted to his men, 'Take a stand men we will all stick together here and fight,' he was also hoping that the other SAS team would have arrived by now, but there has been no sign of them.

The men even the wounded all got ready for the final fight, with what ammunition they had left. About twenty Argentine Marines could be seen closing towards them for the kill, the SAS men started to put down accurate well aimed fire and hitting the advancing Marines, but they knew they were now outnumbered and any minute now they will be overrun by the marines as they closed in towards them.

It was just at the point when the SAS men were now running out of there ammunition and the Argentine Marines were charging towards them, that an immense spread of fire zipped above the SAS men's heads and ripped into the advancing Argentine Marines, Stokesey and his ten SAS men had arrived and were now putting down well aimed bursts of fire onto the advancing Argentine Marines.

With a sudden push back into the Argentine Marines the second SAS team had now started to pull the Mikado team up onto there feet and to head out of the forest. The men had about two kilometres to move towards the main road, they had put a large dent into the Argentine Marines, but they did not realise that the Argentine army had one hundred soldiers in the forest hunting them down and as the SAS men had now started to move out of the forest the Argentinian soldiers were being re grouped to procced with the pursuit.

*

Major Castillo of the 602 Commando company was now running through the forest to get to the front with his Marines, he was furious that they had not stopped any of the SAS men so far, and he wanted to be up front and then take the SAS men before they vanished well inside of Chile.

The Argentine soldiers had their orders to pursue the British soldiers over the border into Chile, but Major Castillo knew they had very little time before the Chilean government, reacted to them being there, and sent their own troops to stop them.

Major Castillo had now caught up with the Argentine troops that were following the SAS men and he had now passed them ordering them to stay behind him and his team of men as they moved forward, and now joined with the other Marines that were on the southern side of the forest and were close to the SAS men, A quick chat with the lieutenant that was in charge of the group of Marines, and Major Castillo was now moving his men around ready to advance quickly on the retreating SAS men.

The SAS men were slowly moving back towards the vehicles at the main road, they were hampered with the fact that they had casualties, three wounded and two dead to carry out with them. Stokesey and his men had replenished the Mikado team with plenty of ammunition, and they had stopped for a few minutes to load up magazines with rounds, the three wounded men had also loaded up with ammunition, as long as they were conscious then they would still fight,

Stokesey could see movement in the corner of his eye, he could see Argentine Marines rushing along the southern side and he knew they were going to try and cut the men off, Stokesey moved his men around, he knew they were going to be coming to an opening soon through the forest, and he knew they would be ambushed as they crossed that opening, Stokesey sent two men forward to get to the opening and have a look at what they will be up against.

They checked the wounded men, Colonel Bradly was not too bad his wound was a round through the muscle, it did not look like it had hit any arteries and it definitely had not hit any bones, Sergeant Major Owen had been hit in the shoulder and the round had passed through and again looked like it had not hit anything important on the way through, Major Austin had taken a round in the stomach and that did look nasty as they knew it was organ damage, but despite the pain he was still mobile.

They patched the wounded up and placed them in the middle of the stick and with Billy and Chack carrying the two dead they, started to make there way west again towards the road. The two men who moved forward were now watching the Argentine Marines taking up a position ready for an ambush, the two SAS men watched the Argentine Marines through there night vision goggles as the Marines took up their final positions.

Stokesey and the rest of the men moved forward slowly, all the time they were watching all around to make sure no one had sneaked in towards them as they headed towards the small break in the forest.

They moved forward slowly, Stokesey moved ahead of the men to make contact with his two men who were watching the Argentine Marines that had set up an ambush just in front of the retreating SAS men.

'Can you see them,' Stokesey asked his two men.

'Yeah, there are four groups one just in front and the other three down towards the south, we have them marked.'

'So how are we going to deal with them,' Stokesey asked.

'203 high explosive on each position and then put down some lead.'

'Good, I will bring the rest of the men up here, then and then we will hit them.'

Stokesey patted the men on the back and slid away keeping down low to the ground, he then went back to the rest of the men who were now watching the rear as they can hear the Argentine soldiers approaching their position.

'Okay lads we have a ambush waiting for us just up in front, we will sneak in low towards the position and then the two guys up front will put some high explosive grenades into the Argies, and we will then follow up by sticking a lot of lead into the positions and hopefully hit some of them, and then we can make a dash across that open bit, and then back into the forest on the other side,' Stokesey took a deep breath, 'now lads it pains me to say it but I think we will be better off leaving our

OPERATION MIKADO

two dead here, we can maybe come back for them later when all this is done.'

The eight men that were left from the Mikado team all looked at each other, they all thought that they would never leave anyone behind but at the moment the two dead are slowing them up.

'Yes, I think it is for the best, we will leave the two men here and return when the coast is clear,' Colonel Bradley said as he backed up Stokesey, in a way that was an order, he had taken it on to himself to make the decision as he knew his men would decide to carry on and carry them. There were sad faces but no arguments, the men pulled the bodies and placed them both side by side in a well covered area and then were ready to fight.

'Okay troops lets move,' Stokesey said as he slid forward on his hands and knees towards the ambush area. The men followed him, and they were now all ready for a fight.

Major Castillo had now organised his Marines into a well thought out ambush position, he was convinced that the SAS men would put down a fire and manoeuvre movement when they exited the forest and run over the open ground.

His men were all waiting, victory would be there's soon, and the SAS men would be captured, he checked his men once more and made sure that they were all ready for battle.

Stokesey and his men reach the area where the two SAS men were watching the Argentine

Marines on the other side of the opening, The Argentine men were well hidden and ready, but the SAS team knew exactly where they had gone in and hidden. The two SAS men had a plan, they would hit each area with a 203 grenade, but one of the men showed Stokesey his 203 star cluster round, it will burn like the sun for seven seconds as it falls to the ground. 'We are going to send one of these up, the brightness from it should glare up there night vision scopes and goggles by surprise, and temporarily blind them, we will then hit them with some 203 grenades, shower them in lead, and make a run across the clearing into the forest on the other side,' the one SAS man said.

'Good plan, I will get the rest of the men ready to move,' Stokesey replied, and he then went back to the men and gave them the plan, so none of the SAS men would use night vision equipment during the attack.

The men moved forward into positions overlooking the opening and towards the Argentine positions, ready to put down some covering fire.

They waited for the star cluster round to be fired, there was a muffled "clump" noise as the grenade was launched, and then it flared with the bright light as it dropped towards the ground, as it did the two men fired off two sets of 203 grenades in towards the Argentine positions, as soon as they had exploded the men poured in a volley of rapid fire into each position, there were rounds bouncing around the trees and even branches dropping from the ferocious fire power being placed onto the Argentine marine positions.

The SAS men had now got ready to run across the opening, and as soon as the seven seconds had passed, and the flare went out they ran hell for leather across the opening.

*

Major Castillo and his men were taken by complete surprise of the attack on there ambush position, all his men were waiting for the SAS men to appear from the forest and move across the open area in front of them, the Argentine Marines were all equipped with night vision equipment and were confident that they would have a good kill zone in front. However, they never expected the flare and when it illuminated everything in front it made there night vision equipment white out and useless.

The volley of fire from the SAS was so intense that Major Castillo had lost half of his men in the counter ambush.

*

The SAS men now have only two kilometres to go, and then they will reach the road and their vehicles, they have left a handful of well armed men with the vehicles keeping watch to make sure no one interferes with a getaway, the Argentine soldiers have now been slowly reduced but there are still a large amount out in the forest hunting them, and now they are all being directed in against the SAS men.

The SAS men now have a large amount of ammunition thanks to Stokesey and his team who had come with a large supply of ammunition ready just in case. The men know they will have to make a stand at some point as they will be vulnerable when they get to the vehicles, they may well have to make a stand before then and take the fight in towards the Argentinians who are in a hot pursuit.

The men go through there ammunition and reload the magazines to make sure they have all got enough ammunition, they then start to move forward a little bit quicker, Colonel Bradley checked his watch it was now 06.20, they have been in the forest for a lot longer than he had thought, and now he was now concerned with the light as they are now seeing a kind of twilight that has brightened up the area slightly, it was enough to notice things moving in an eerie way like shadows.

Every now and then the men would be on the receiving end of some shots that are being fire from the forest behind them, the rounds were 7.62 so the men knew they were from conscript troops firing there FN rifles, but they also knew that the 7.62 round could be fatal if it hit them.

The men would return fire on any troops that opened up on them and with the SAS men their fire was well aimed shots, and they were slowly hitting the Argentine soldiers, not only that but the SAS men had a large amount of 203

OPERATION MIKADO

grenades that they were sending through the trees towards the Argentine soldiers, and this was keeping them down until they were ordered to advance again.

Stokesey had now stopped the men in their tracks, and now they had all got down prone on the ground, the vehicles that Stokesey and his men had arrived in were parked up on the other side of the main road, and that is where they are heading towards, inside another forest area.

However, the men who stayed with the vehicles had seen a number of Argentine army vehicles stop just south of the position that they were hiding in on the main road, it would seem that the Argentine soldiers must have crossed the border further south and have now headed up here to join the fight, the only good news is that they are conscripted soldiers and not Marines. But they were still a problem that had to be dealt with.

It was now confirmed that there were three vehicles, with a total of about twenty men, and they had pulled up by the side of the road near the edge of the forest, the SAS team with their vehicles had however two GPMG machine guns with them and have now made them ready to put down fire on the three vehicles and the men around them.

Stokesey had now worked out that he was about one kilometre from the road and the last thing he would want was to run into the men from the three vehicles so the SAS men with the vehicles have now checked that there are no Chilian civil-

193

ians in the area and have got there two GPMG guns into position, and they have now opened fire on the twenty men and the three vehicles.

The clear view for the SAS, GPMG crews had meant that they had put down a good, sustained fire onto the Argentine men and the vehicles, they had hit at least half of the men and have put substantial damage into the three vehicles that carried them here, in fact one has now caught fire and is burning well on the side of the road.

The rest of the Argentine soldiers had run off into the forest to escape the fire from the two GPMG guns, the SAS crew that are with there vehicles that fired the guns had now ceased firing, but they were now making their guns ready just in case any Argentine forces burst out from the forest.

Stokesey along with both his team and the Mikado team were now only eight hundred metres from the edge of the forest, but they were still coming under fire from behind them, and this was making their progress more difficult and slow, it was now that they had decided they would make a stand and let the Argentine soldiers come at them, they were all equipped with plenty of ammunition and they were all now ready for a good fire fight, the only one that would probably not be able to fight was Major Austin who was now in a bad shape from his wound to the stomach.

The men spread themselves out into small groups ready for the onslaught of Argentine troops, they had everything ready and watched on as small shadows appeared in front of them inside the forest, the men all knew that they would have to let the enemy come too them so that they could deal a maximum blow to them.

Slowly the Argentine troops moved towards them, they were now out at one hundred metres and with the twilight they could just make them all out, they let them move towards them, eighty metres then seventy meters, the closer they came the less cover they would have, the SAS man had their fingers on their triggers as they allowed the Argentine soldiers too close in on them, they all lay prone ready and waiting, fifty metres and they still held.

It was at thirty metres that the SAS soldiers opened fire ripping through magazines of ammunition firing almost point blank into the Argentine soldiers who were caught out totally unaware of the ambush that was waiting for them, some Argentine soldiers had managed to return fire but they were cut down mercilessly by the SAS rifle fire, not only that but the SAS men also managed to fire a barrage of 203 grenades into the forest and onto the advancing Argentinian men and these grenades were also cutting them down.

What was left of the advancing Argentine army was now on the retreat and they were now running back towards the east to try and regroup into another force. Stokesey and the Mikado team kept the pressure on the enemy and even started to stand and move towards them firing well aimed rounds towards them. The Argentinians had never seen or ever thought that they would ever see an onslaught like it, and the ones that were not hit in the fire fight or never got the chance to run away with the others, had now thrown down there weapons and had their hands in the air in surrender.

Stokesey and his team just watched the Argentines as they wandered around with there hands up, Stokesey could not take any prisoners, so they just stood with there weapons pointed at the Argentinians who now slowly turned and moved away back towards their own border.

CHAPTER FOURTEEN.

Northwood.

There was still no signal from the Mikado team that was on the ground inside of Chile, there was also no information from Stokesey and his team, the last that Northwood had heard was that the teams inside of Chile were on there way to meet the Mikado team and bring them back.

The Prime Minister was awaiting any good news before she announced the success of the mission to the public, but now some news had been creeping out from Buenos Aries that a British attack on there soil has been prevented by the Argentine forces, and the press who have the news are now putting pressure on the Prime Minister to release a news statement.

Pressure was now on the men of the special forces operations at Northwood, they were also awaiting any kind of news to come in.

'Maybe they did not blow the Exocets up,' Colonel Thomas was saying as he paced up and down the ops room awaiting any incoming news.

'They must have done, unless the Argentinians moved the explosives before they went off,' Colonel Cedric was saying.

The Director was now in the room, and he too was pacing up and down awaiting a response on the radio. The tension was mounting by the minute but still no answer, and then the telephone had rung and made everyone jump and then someone answered the phone and called the Director over 'it is for you sir.'

The Director had answered the call and placed the phone down, he took a deep breath 'I will not be long, the Minister is here and wants to see me urgently,' he said as he left the ops room, this added even more tension, maybe he has some real bad news everyone thought.

The Director entered the small room where the Minister was waiting with one of his men, they were both pacing the office, and both looked like they had just received bad news.

The Minister was the first to speak, 'Ah, there you are,' he said as he took in a deep breath and continued, 'have you received any news from the Mikado team that are still on the ground.'

'No Minister, we are still waiting.'

'Hmm, well I have just had the Chilean ambassador on the line, it seems that there is some kind of battle going on near the border with Argentina, he said that he will have to order some troops into the area to bring it under control.'

'That may well be our men.'

The Minister shook his head 'Damn it this may well cause an international incident, something that we wanted to avoid.'

'Well with all due respect Minister, it is Argentina that has invaded Chile not the United Kingdom.'

The Minister was taken back by the remark and then stormed out of the office, the Director now made his way back to the ops room, 'have I missed anything.'

'Nothing as yet,' Colonel Cedric replied.

'Damn it, why does no one report in to us.'

The Prime Minister was now made aware of the situation at a meeting with other Ministers that were discussing the war in the South Atlantic, at this moment in time she decided to ignore the fact that there was some kind of problem in Chile, but she would call President Pinochet as soon as possible to offer her regrets that Argentina had in fact invaded Chile in the pursuit of her men, the good news was that the Exocet threat was now almost erased, and that was good news, however there was still anxiety over the recent reports that the Exocet missiles were in fact not destroyed by the SAS team, and this was something that had also started to worry the Prime Minister.

*

Major Castillo still had a small team of men that were still attempting to cut off the escaping SAS team, who were now moving through the forest towards the road. Fire and smoke could now be seen at the edge of the forest and Castillo was now aware that the burning was an Argentine vehicle that had been damaged in an ambush, he also concluded that there must be even more British forces here than he had thought. Castillo had thought this through, in his mind he knew that he could not fight even more British troops if they were responsible for the damage of the vehicles.

However, Castillo was not one to give up that easy and he continued to order his men to head west towards the road in an attempt to cut down the SAS men as they escape towards the road.

There was one more chance and that was for Major Castillo to take his men along the banks of the Uribe river in one last attempt too take them out. Castillo pulled his men away from the forest and got them all too clamber down the river bank, they would then use the river bank to provide cover as they moved west towards the road and then they could put down their fire onto the SAS men when they emerge from the trees of the forest.

The men got down and were now moving through the river itself, it was not in flood so the water at this time was not so deep, and the men made rapid progress under cover towards the main road.

Once the Argentine Marines along with a handful of conscripts, had reached an open area, that was west of the forest, and looked out onto the area from the south, Castillo halted his men, and positioned them all along the river bank. At anytime now the SAS men would emerge from the forest and have to move across the area to the north of Castillo's position, and now Castillo and his men were in a good position to ambush them.

Stokesey was now leading the men out of the forest and towards the main road, so far, they had not come under any fire for a while from the rear, so they were now confident that they had no one following them now, however Stokesey was not so convinced that the Marines had given up on the pursuit and he was even more cautious and stayed on full alert, there was no time to relax.

Stokesey and his team had come to the start of an opening and then they had a two hundred meter opening too cross to get to the vehicles that were parked at the main road, somehow Stokesey had a feeling that they were going to be ambushed as they crossed over the open space, and he knew this of all places would be the ideal spot.

The men halted at the edge of the trees just before the wide opening. There was no other way across this area, they would have to cross over it, the men looked through there night vision to see if they could see any enemy soldiers out there but so far, they could not see anything, the only thing visible was the burning Argentine vehicle too there left.

Stokesey radioed in to his men with the vehicles and asked them if they could see anything out there and they reported they could see nothing on the flat space.

'Maybe they are not there, laddie,' Billy Ballantine suggested.

'No there out there somewhere, I can feel it,'

Colonel Bradley managed to hop his way over to have a look and see, 'are you sure they would be out there,' he asked.

'Yes, boss believe me I know the bastards will be out there ready for us,' Stokesey replied as he continued to look. The light was starting to get slightly brighter now and objects could be seen better, it was at this point that Chack was watching over and he said, 'what is that about one hundred meters to the south it looks like a track or something.'

The men all straining their eyes and all of them looked over at what Chack had indicated too them, 'that looks like a brook or a small river,' Paddy Kelly said as he looked on.

'That is where they are then,' Stokesey answered.

Stokesey knew they would be around somewhere, and this was the best place for them to launch a good ambush they had the flat ground and they had significant cover from the river banks, they could launch a fierce attack on Stokesey and his men.

'What now,' one of the SAS men asked.

Stokesey in the meantime was looking

around, there was one way out and that was to go back into the forest and head north and come out at the top of the opening at five hundred metres up, the vehicles could then come and pick them up from up there, but he thought we could give them one more fight.

'Well lads, we can go back into the wood, and then head north up the trees for another five hundred metres, and then head across up there over to the road, and then meet up with the vehicles, as long as the Argies don't shoot the vehicles up as they leave,' he took a long breath and looked at the men and could see they were awaiting the plan "B". 'Or we could get the vehicle team to put down a shit load of GPMG fire on the bastards and we could then come out of here and fight our way across the two hundred metres to the other side, and then get in the vehicles and bugger off into Chile.'

Stokesey let the idea hang for a moment then looked at the men, they all gave him a direct answer, 'we will fight here,' each man answered.

'Colonel, I want to apologise I should have asked you first,' Stokesey said as he had forgotten how the Colonel and Major Austin had out ranked him,' Colonel Bradley put his hand up as to brush it off 'you carry on Sergeant Stokes, myself and Major Austin and of course the Sergeant Major are in no fit state to give orders.'

'Thank you, sir.'

Stokesey got on to his radio and called up the guys with the vehicles and gave them the plan. The men with the vehicles had set up there two GPMG machine guns on the edge of some trees that were by the road and overlooked the small river, they would give full covering fire when ready, Stokesey had again organised his men so that the wounded men were in the middle and although they were wounded, they could also put down some fire but they would also be protected by the group as they crossed the open land.

The light had now started to increase it was just gone 07.00 when Colonel Bradley looked at his watch.

'Ready boys,' Stokesey whispered, and he watched as he had a thumbs up from the rest of his team, they were now good to go.

Major Castillo and his men were also a bit uncomfortable as they had been stood in running cold water for a while waiting for anything to happen, and then as the light had increased slightly, they could see movement to there right, it was the SAS men moving out from the trees, Major Castillo shouted to his men 'Fuego' and his men started to open fire.

But just as Major Castillo had given his order, he had exposed his position and the two GPMG gun that were over to the left had now identified them, and they had now opened fire on the Argentine position. The two GPMG's converged there fire along the river bank and at the same time the SAS team had now made there move from the trees and were now moving across the two hundred metre open land towards the trees at the side of the open ground, the men were executing a fire and manoeuvre movement that every infantryman would know and this movement becomes second nature, while one half moves the other half puts down covering fire, and all the time the two GPMG,s keep putting down an onslaught of covering fire from the side.

The SAS men were now making fast movement over the open land and the two GPMG's were keeping up a barrage of controlled bursts of fire keeping the enemy down in their cover.

Major Castillo and his men were now down behind the river bank the immense fire was ripping the top of the river bank apart as rounds after rounds hammered down over them, chunks of mud were now falling into the river around their feet, there was no way anyone could put there head up to see what was going on the incoming fire was so fierce. Major Castillo was now cursing, five of his men were now face down in the river and floating past him as they had been caught in the heavy fire.

The SAS men had made it across the opening and were now onto the main road and towards the vehicles. The two GPMG, s were still pumping dozens of rounds over towards the river while the men were all loaded up into the three vans, eventually the GPMG, s slowed up there firing as the men withdrew from there position, and then jumped up into the rear of the vans with the red hot barrels of there GPMG, s still smoking as they started too cool down in the rear of the van.

*

Major Castillo looked up as soon as the shooting had finished, he then climbed out of the river and ran across the flat open ground towards the road, only to see the vans driving off down the road, Castillo was just about to open fire on the last van when a large truck came into view and forced him to abort his shooting.

'Well men, we have done it,' Major Bradley said as he stretched his wounded leg out, he looked over towards Major Austin who was now in a bit of a bad state, 'what about Major Austin,' Colonel Bradley asked.

'Don't worry boss, we will have him in a hospital within the hour,' one of the men answered. The vans drove along the main route at a steady speed, and headed north towards the main route 257 where they then headed west for a few miles where they then came to a stop.

A Chilian army helicopter was on the ground and waiting for them to arrive, the helicopter would take the three wounded men to a Military hospital where their wounds could be seen too.

Colonel Bradley, Sergeant Major Owen and Major Austin, were all transferred from the van to the helicopter, and then the men on the ground watched as the helicopter made its way up into the sky and headed away, the men then climbed back into the vans and headed towards Porvenir and the ferry to take them to Punta Arenas.

*

Meanwhile Major Castillo and his remaining men had now checked out the two remaining vehicles that were on the roadside, the third vehicle was ablaze, but the flames were now dying down, they managed to start the two vehicles, and would return in these to the border crossing just south of there position. The other remaining Argentine troops were now retreating back towards the border and taking as much of there dead and wounded and equipment as they could carry.

The Chilean army had arrived in the area and had orders too look for the two bodies of Captain Rasheed and Sergeant Williams that were left inside the forest, it took them a fair while to locate the bodies but they did find them quickly, they also collected a number of dead Argentine soldiers and a lot of abandoned equipment, and even took a few Argentine prisoners.

The bodies of Captain Rasheed and Sergeant Williams would be flown direct to Santiago and handed over to the British embassy for repatriation to the United Kingdom. The Argentine Prisoners were returned direct to the border crossing at Paso San Sebastian along with any dead Argentine troops that were found, all equipment was retained by the Chilian army.

Stokesey and his team had now sent a message back to Northwood that the Mikado team had now been picked up but there were casualties with

JOEY HOGAN

two dead and three wounded.

CHAPTER FIFTEEN.

Northwood.

The ops room came alive when they had received the message that the Mikado team had all been accounted for but there were casualties. The news was transferred direct to the Director, who then made his way direct to a government meeting to inform the Prime Minister of the news.

'Prime Minister, I would like to inform you that the remaining ten men from operation Mikado are now across the border and are now safe inside Chile,' the Director paused for a moment before he continued, 'however I would also wish to inform you that we had taken casualties with two men killed in action and three men wounded, the wounded are in care at a military hospital inside of Chile and are being well looked after.'

The Prime Minister sat silent for a moment as the news sunk in. before she replied.

'Thank you for that news, and my heart goes out to the men who have given their lives and the men who have been wounded,' the Prime Minster said, but her face remained solemn at the news of the casualties, and she also had a question, 'we have also been informed by certain members of the press that the Exocet missiles were not destroyed during the raid, can you shed some light on these reports.'

'Prime Minister, I will get the destruction confirmed as soon as possible.'

'Thank you, we will await your news by return.'

The Director, had now returned too Northwood with the news that the Exocets may well have not been destroyed, 'Colonel Cedric,' he shouted as he entered the rooms of the special forces operations.

Colonel Cedric and Colonel Thomas made their way to the Directors office and entered; the Director was sat behind his desk waiting for them. 'I have just been in a meeting with the Prime Minister and her Ministers, and she has informed me that some members of the press are saying that the Exocets were not destroyed in the raid.'

Cedric was rubbing his chin and thinking, 'well we will have to confirm it with the Mikado team,' he checked his watch, 'the two Hercules are still in the air at the moment returning to Accension so we cannot confirm it with the teams onboard just yet, I will send a message out to men in Chile to try and get some kind of confirmation.'

'It seems like the story has come from Argentina, that they pulled the detonators out from the explosives,' the Director said as he looked at the notes handed to him, 'is this possible.'

'It is possible, but our explosive guys usually have some kind of back up plan just in case they do that,' Colonel Thomas replied.

'Well check it out we need to know one way or another,'.

The two Colonels left the office and made there way back to the ops room and prepared a signal to be sent to the team in Chile.

*

Stokesley received the message while the vans were at Porvenir waiting for the ferry.

'Billy, come here,' Stokesey shouted across to Billy Ballantine, Stokesey waited for Billy to come down from his van at the rear of their convoy.

'You called me laddie.'

'Northwood have sent a message about the Exocets, did they blow up, as the Argies are claiming that they removed the explosives.'

'Aye, as far as I know they blew up, Paddy Kelly did the explosives, we will have to ask him,' Billy started looking around for Paddy. 'Hey Paddy come here,' Billy shouted as Billy waved his hand calling Paddy over, and then Paddy started to walk towards them.

'Yeah, what do you want,' Paddy asked.

'Did you put the explosives onto the Exocets,' Stokesey asked.

'Yep.'

'The Argies are saying that they pulled the detonators out and they saved the missiles.'

Paddy Laughed as he replied 'Well, whoever tried to pull the detonator out would have gone up in smoke with the missiles because I placed a booby trap on them just in case, I placed a couple of anti-tamper detonators in there as well so if they were pulled the lot would go up so either way those missiles went bang,' Paddy said with a smile.

Stokesey and Billy knew full well that when it came to explosives Paddy was there main man, he would not only set the explosives, but he will also think what can happen in the time they have been set until the time they go off. Paddy would almost without asking set a secondary device on the explosives to prevent them from being saved.

Stokesey smiled and sent his message back to Northwood, *'Argentinians are talking a load of bollocks, those Exocets were all blown up, end of story.'*

The message was now received at Northwood and handed to Colonel Cedric who then read it out to the Director, 'a message from our men in Chile, Argentinians are talking a load of Bollocks, those Exocets were all blown up, end of story.'

*

The Director had a slight smile on his face when he was told the news, 'I do not somehow think I should tell the Prime Minister the news in those words.' He replied.

'No Sir best not too,'

The Director had now got up and made his way to number ten so that he could update the Prime Minister with the news. Some papers had already started there print with the news that the raid was foiled, and they now had their feet kicked from under them with the incorrect story, when the Prime Minister held a brief news conference on the doorstep of number ten.

'I have just received the news, that a daring raid by members of our very own Special Air Service on the Rio Grande airbase on the mainland of Argentina, to destroy the deadly Exocet missiles, and destroy the aircraft that were being used to launch them, has been a complete success. Our boys are now safe and accounted for, and I will leave you all with this wonderful news.'

As always, the Prime Minister left the statement like it was, and walked back into number ten, and ignored any questions from the press.

In Northwood they were still awaiting news on the two Hercules aircraft that had still to return to Accension Island, the latest news was that the two aircraft had completed there final refuel and were now on their way in towards the island and should reach Ascension Island around midday.

The news that the Exocets at Rio Grande had been destroyed was warmly welcomed by the fleet, they can now rest a little more easy knowing that the deadly threat to all the ships that the missiles had posed, had now been eliminated, but they still had the threat from the low flying Argentine pilots who could still attack with conventional bombs, and still cause substantial damage to the ships.

Other SAS Missions on the mainland were still on the table and with a team watching Rio Gallegos air base, there were now plans being placed on the table for a joint SBS and SAS raid on the airbase and again target the aircraft, and any ordinance that were on the base, however political pressure, and the fact that the fleet had now started to move in towards the Falkland islands and the troops were now being placed onshore, it was decided that this plan should be put on hold.

The men of the Mikado team in Chile were moved out as soon as possible and transported to Santiago where they then travelled back to the UK for their debrief at Hereford. But their trip back was diverted over the United States and then they found themselves inside a huge C5 transport aircraft on a flight back to Ascension.

Colonel Thomas was now called in to see the Director and knew that he would face some severe wrath for his secret mission.

'You wanted to see me Brigadier,' Colonel Thomas said as he entered the office at Northwood.

'Yes Bill, please take a seat.'

Colonel Thomas sat the other side of the small desk that the Director used at Northwood and waited his fate.

'What you had done went against everything we expect within the Regiment, you went against what everyone had thought was the best, and a direct way forward, by putting a single man behind the lines to prove your own point.'

Colonel Thomas, looked up at the ceiling, his intention was to never go against anyone, he just wanted a plan that would have worked, and that the men who were taking the risk were not all sacrificed for a failed mission, a failed fantasy dream.

'I have nothing too say Sir, I only wanted to make sure that we did not waste the lives of good men on a mission that would have failed. If we would have sent those two Hercules into Rio Grande with what we know now they would have been both shot up on the runway before the men had got even out of them.'

The Brigadier General sat back in his chair and looked at Colonel Thomas, 'If we ever have a next time, and a plan that you do not like, for Gods sake come forward and put your idea to us, we have all had a wake up call and we have had a success, but like you explained it could have gone wrong,' the Brigadier General took a deep breath as he thought a little bit more, 'well the mission worked, thanks to your one man on the ground, now go back to Hereford and debrief them, we need to learn as much from this as we can for the future.'

'Will that be all Sir.'
'Yes, carry on Colonel.'
'Thank you, Sir.'
And at that Colonel Thomas stood and left

JOEY HOGAN

the office.

CHAPTER SIXTEEN.

Bradbury Lines Hereford.

Colonel Thomas had returned to Hereford and awaited the men to all return to base for a debrief.

The Hercules had landed at Accension island, and the men were given twenty four hours off, the plan was to return them to Hereford for their de brief, but there was a war on, and they were now destined to take on more missions in the South Atlantic.

Major Austin however was still in Chile being looked after; he was not passed as fit to return so he would have another few weeks there. However, Colonel Bradley and Sergeant Major Owen returned home to Hereford.

Stokesey and his men were still in and out on various missions inside of Argentina, but with the war now being fought on the Falkland Islands, everything was expected to be ended soon.

Colonel Thomas and Colonel Cedric were

now conducting a debrief of the mission and everything that had happened that night. Also present in the debrief were the crew of the RAF Hercules transport aircraft that took the SAS men into Argentina, a lot was learnt from the mission and a lot of pressure would have to be placed on future governments to provide better kit all around not only for the SAS men but also for the crews and men of 47 Squadron RAF who carry out the special forces flights.

The mission was a gamble, but it had paid off by the determination of the men and the RAF crews working together.

I dedicate this book to Len
Happy reading Len, enjoy the storey.

I also dedicate this book to all the men from across all the services who sailed down to the South Atlantic during those troubled times in 1982. These men worked together and showed how all services can come together to make an unbeatable force.

Copyright, Joey Hogan 2021

Printed in Great Britain
by Amazon